RIDGELY GREATHOUSE

*Confederate, Conspirator,
Convict, and Capitalist*

Marisue Burleson Potts

Ridgely Greathouse
Confederate, Conspirator, Convict, and Capitalist
Marisue Burleson Potts © 2021

Danella Reno Dickson, Research Contributor
Book Production by Aloha Publishing, AlohaPublishing.com
Cover and Interior Design by Fusion Creative Works, FusionCW.com

Print ISBN: 978-1-7356605-1-6
eBook ISBN: 978-1-7356605-2-3

Published by Mollie Burleson Ranch Ltd.

Printed in the United States of America

To the past and current members of
Stephen W. Wilkinson Chapter 1943
United Daughters of the Confederacy
Organized and Chartered 1927
Lubbock, Texas

Contents

Illustrations

About This Book

"No man is an island, entire of itself; every man is a piece of the continent, a part of the main . . . any man's death diminishes me, because I am involved in mankind; and therefore never send to know for whom the bells tolls; it tolls for thee."

—John Donne

If there are lessons to be learned from the epic struggle of Ridgely Greathouse to satisfy his ambitions and live a meaningful life, only one published interview has been found that might shed light on how he thought and what motivated him. James O'Meara, the editor of the *Idaho World* in Idaho City, Idaho, recounted the successes of the Greathouse brothers due to their diligence, shrewdness, performance, and good business practices. He described Ridge as bright, witty, intelligent, and both charming and mannerly. O'Meara attributed Ridge's desperate and disloyal designs of a conspiracy to the encouragement and companionship of those of a similar nature. From Ridge's early days as a messenger carrying gold dust over dangerous country, he operated in a daring, fearless manner without concern for the consequences.

The enigma of Ridge Greathouse posits certain questions. In the light of being a supporter of the Southern Confederacy, was he a patriot, or was he a traitor only because the North prevailed? Was he a traitor to the Confederacy, even though Asbury Harpending had a blank letter of marque to legitimize the piracy, because they stood to profit? Was he a conspirator only to become a capitalist? Was being a capitalist the driving force behind all his actions? Read the stories that follow and make your own determination.

Although more in the media's eye than most citizens, Ridge Greathouse's experiences were not unlike those of many other Southerners: trials for conspiracy, arrest or re-arrest without habeas corpus, federal imprisonment as a political prisoner, flight from the United States, exile and relocation in foreign countries, and the long process of being pardoned or not, with its vagaries and uncertainties and corruption.

The time of turmoil before the Civil War juxtaposed opposing views and conflicting loyalties to family and culture which were not confined just to the South, but also to border states like Kentucky and the Western Territories. The Civil War was precipitated by cultural and geographical differences, disparity in available natural resources and manpower, a conflict over states' rights versus federal power, industrial versus agrarian, and planter society versus urban elite. These were in addition to the humanitarian element of hold-ing people against their will without compensation or recompense, or freeing them without preparation, education, or direction. No matter the sectional differences, there were good people and those we deemed bad or detrimental to society. No matter their code of ethics, there were the rich, the middle class, and the poor—the poverty-stricken and the hopeless.

A Confederate first and always, Ridge Greathouse threw himself, heart and soul, into the South's cause in his own way. Long after his passing, in 2011 the Plemons Chapter of the United Sons of the Confederacy and the Stephen W. Wilkinson Chapter of the United Daughters of the Confederacy honored and acknowledged Ridge Greathouse for his contributions. Who knows what adventures, struggles, and triumphs might have led him through life's twisting trails? In the case of Ridge Greathouse, ambition, the temptation of quick profits, and exploitation played their parts. However, no man should be judged by his last days. The stories that follow document, to the best of my ability, the adventurous path of Ridge Greathouse's life, ending in a quiet cemetery on the Rolling Plains of Texas.

— Marisue Burleson Potts, 2021

Prologue

On a small hill east of the ranching community of Matador in Motley County, Texas, lies East Mound Cemetery. On 10 acres of land donated by the Matador Land and Cattle Company, Ltd., of Dundee, Scotland, 28 Confederate veterans rest there. When the Scottish syndicate's secretary, Alexander Mackay, was approached by local citizens with a plea to purchase a section of land for a burying ground, he dismissed the idea by saying, "A square mile solely as a burying ground gives a bad impression of the climate."[1] To the contrary, the Rolling Plains and the Caprock foothills began as early as 1879 to attract veterans of the ravished Confederate States of America (CSA) with opportunities for a new start and a chance to buy cheap land.

Among the CSA veterans in the cemetery were notables such as J.M. Campbell, brother to Henry H. Campbell, founder of the original Matador Cattle Company; J.T. "Pat" Cornett, the builder of the 1891 jail; Mose Damron, a frontier scout and Indian fighter;

---

1. Pearce, W. M. *The Matador Land and Cattle Company* (Norman: University of Oklahoma, 1964), p. 55.

A.M. Turner and H.H. Harris, medical doctors; John Waybourn, Texas Ranger; Charles Wideman, Union conscript, who at age 17 defected to serve in the Confederate Home Guard; and Philander Cribbs, an Alabama farmer who introduced the cotton culture to the first settlers of the Matador area.

Philander Cribbs

As a boy, Philander Cribbs joined his family in the gold rush exodus to California by sailing from Mobile, Alabama, crossing the Isthmus of Panama by mule, and then sailing to California to mine for gold. Upon their return to Alabama, his father, Daniel Cribbs, used his profit to buy slaves to work in their pottery factory. Crossing the Isthmus again, Philander Cribbs returned to California for four years, but he made it back to Alabama and married just weeks before his state seceded from the Union. Philander, as second lieutenant in Company K of the 20th Alabama Infantry regiment, served in Kentucky, Mississippi, and Georgia, and suffered many hardships, including being captured twice.[2]

In addition to Cribbs and those early settlers of the county, another 15 CSA veterans either lived in Motley County but were buried elsewhere, like Henry H. Campbell; or their widows applied for a pension from the county; or they belonged to the local chapter of the United Veterans of the Confederacy, Camp S.B. Maxey No. 860. The gatherings of Camp Maxey's veterans were held under the cottonwoods near the South Pease waterfall in Roaring Springs, so named by buffalo hunter Frank Collinson for the generous flow

---

2. Potts, Marisue, "P.A. Cribbs, An Infantryman in a 'Modern' War." (Senior Research paper for Dr. Alwyn Barr's Civil War History Class 4304, Texas Tech University, Oct. 24, 1997); "Philander Cribbs" file, Motley County Museum, 828 Dundee St., Matador, Texas, 79244.

from the Ogallala aquifer. The informal assemblies spawned the Old Settlers Reunion, an event still celebrated annually at the village of Roaring Springs.

1. United Veterans of the Confederacy of Camp S.B. Maxey, No. 860. Philander Cribbs is first on the left of the front row.

Cribbs took an active role in the affairs of Camp Maxey and assumed responsibility to see that the graves of the members who served in Texas, Missouri, Georgia, Mississippi, Alabama, North Carolina, and Virginia were marked by the CSA Southern Cross. In a letter to the Confederated Southern Memorial Association, he wrote in 1925, "We have here in our small cemetery 17 soldiers without a marker and some without a stone . . . All of them were good, true Confederate soldiers except three. Two were Indian scouts for Confederate troops in Texas, the other a noted character, Ridgeland (sic) Greathouse." Cribbs went on to describe Greathouse's service to the Confederacy as "a great deed unrecognized because of the sacrifice made by a noble soul."[3]

Over 150 years after the Civil War, we know little about why the South felt justified in seceding. Nor do we contemplate the consequences that devasting national event wreaked on individuals. Many people in the South did not own slaves or necessarily support the institution of slavery, yet individuals, county officials, and governors who served the Confederacy were threatened with consequences so severe, they considered exile and relocation to foreign lands to escape them. Looking at this one individual, who did support the economic benefits of slavery but whose family had only a few slaves, we find his life testified that we are shaped by our upbringing, social conditions, environment, and the friends we choose. With this thought, I offer the incredible story of Ridgely Greathouse.

---

3. "CSMA Notes," *Confederate Veteran* Vol. 33. (Confederated Southern Memorial Association: 1925), p. 353.

CHAPTER 1

End of the Trail

No doubt, Greathouse was a "noted character," but his later years were not his best ones. As he roamed the vast Matador Land and Cattle Company, he eked out a living by poisoning or trapping skunks, wolves, coyotes, and prairie dogs, and skinning them for their pelts.

Duff Green, a regional grassroots historian, recorded many stories about the cowboys, settlers, and characters in the ranch country of the Rolling Plains of Motley, Cottle, Dickens, Kent, and King counties. Green assembled an insightful description of Ridge Greathouse, one filtered down through generations of cowboy tales.

On a Big Chief Tablet with a lead pencil, Duff recorded the following:

In the 1880s, Ridge Greathouse was found on the Matador Ranch, where he labored as poisoner and trapper of predatory animals. He was often mentioned, out of his hearing, as the Old Skunk Skinner. It was never conceded that he drew a salary from the Matador Ranch. He had a light spring wagon, a couple of small Spanish mules, and his bed and camp outfit. The Matador furnished him chuck, and in fact usually during the working season, he could be found camped with the Matador wagon and ate with them during those times. His remuneration was the pelts of his kill, possibly an added bounty for lobo wolves and panthers, and he got the beef hides, which meant a hide every day or so.

In the winter, he went it alone, moving and camping at his pleasure. The varmints were thick and found almost everywhere, and he knew how to get them. He usually sold his furs and beef hides whenever circumstances justified. He had little need of money, other than to obtain a few rough work clothes, strychnine, traps, and the like to cover his incidental expenses. This left ample money for periodical sprees to drown his troubled mind. Often some of the boys hooked his wet goods and drank it themselves.

On one such occasion, as Ridge Greathouse was sobering up a bit while reading poetry, he laid his book aside and said, "If the gentleman who stole my whiskey will step out and make acknowledgment of the fact, I will fill him so full of lead he won't be able to walk up the hill." Silence reigned in his hearing, so he turned to reading his book again.

He was then an old, old man, with hair as white as snow and a beard that was thin, straggly, and grey. He simply went his way, to and fro about the country with his camp equipage and possibly a worn and dog-eared copy of *William Shakespeare* or Homer's Greek *Iliad* as company, trapping, poisoning, and skinning wild animals for their pelts.

Ridge Greathouse seemed to shun houses or shelters, for he constantly camped in the open. His clothes were torn and tattered, dirty and greasy, and often laced together with twine to shear off the icy winds that blew across his pathway.

As the country settled up, Ridge Greathouse became a thorn in the flesh of all lovers and owners of dogs, because much of the poison he scattered over his wolf drags was left behind to kill the dogs that found it. Indirectly, Uncle

Ridge got a good many dogs – he guessed a thousand – and said the owners always claimed they were worth at least a $100 apiece.[4]

Greathouse was a man of contrasts who dressed the part of an apparent derelict but easily quoted Latin phrases and classical literature, and he presented a puzzle. Despite his filthy clothes, stiff with blood and grease, Greathouse meticulously undertook a daily cleansing in even the rawest weather, sometimes chopping a hole in the ice of a stream to skinny-dip. Although in his past he had known privilege and grandiose schemes, he lived on the open range in his wagon or a dirty tent. He was sharp of tongue and crusty in exterior, but he had moments of compassion, as evidenced by taking up with a stray like himself.

One of the accounts handed down by the cowboys was recorded by the Matador Ranch manager's son, Harry H. Campbell. The story claimed that a waif from Kansas City, escaping abusive or dishonest uncles, showed up on the cattle range, longing to be a cowboy. Seizing the moment, Uncle Ridge added young Billy Parks to his lonely cross-country critter-killing sprees.

Before long, the manager of the Pitchfork Ranch, D.B. Gardner, stepped in on behalf of the boy and offered him a chance to get some schooling and work on a ranch. The schooling didn't take, but the cowboying did. The kid, whose real name of Billy Partlow was later revealed to Gardner on a trip to St. Louis, became an accomplished hand on the Pitchfork Ranch. Later, when he worked on

---

4. Green, John Duff. *Recollections* (Roaring Springs, Texas; Joan Green Lawrence, editor, 1988), pp. 259-261.

the Matador Ranch, he was known simply as the "Pitchfork Kid"[5] to Ridge and the cowboys on the range.

However, it was the presence of the enigmatic Uncle Ridge Greathouse around the campfires of the Matador Ranch that led the cowboys to great speculation. Who was this man? Where did he come from? How had he spent his life? Where was he educated? What "great deed of sacrifice" did he undertake in the Civil War? What lost love or exploits isolated him from society? For the answers, we must start at the beginning, in the territory of Kentucky.

---

5. Campbell, Harry H. *The Early History of Motley County* (Nortex Press, Austin, 1958), pp. 41-42.

2. Wolfer. Art by Kayla White.

CHAPTER 2

Kentucky, Borderland of Strife

Ridgely Greathouse was born in 1831 in Mason County, Kentucky, to William and Jane Lewis Greathouse. Both the Greathouse family and the Lewis family were deeply rooted in the Ohio River frontier at his birth. Greathouse blood had long been shed on Kentucky soil, beginning with Ridgely's relative Jonathan Greathouse.[6]

Jonathan Greathouse, a military captain, was on his way to the village of Limestone in Mason County on March 24, 1791, with a festive party of settlers looking to relocate. While traveling down the major transportation corridor of the Ohio River, their slow-moving flatboats, powered only by oars, were attacked by Indians. A defense formed but those on the water were at a disadvantage. Apparently it was a planned attack because Jonathan's older brother, Daniel Greathouse, had led the Yellow Creek Massacre during Lord Dunmore's War of 1774.[7] That blitz resulted in the killing of the

---

6. "Jonathan Greathouse (1766-1791)," "Gabriel Greathouse (1761-1829)," Ancestry Family Trees, Provo, Utah. ancestry.com

7. "Lord Dunmore's War—1774" and "James Logan, American Indian Leader," *Encyclopaedia Britannica*, accessed on April 18, 2020: https://www.britannica.com/event/Lord-Dunmores-War; https://www.britannica.com/biography/James-Logan-American-Indian-leader

family of the war leader of the Iroquois-allied Mingo tribe, James Logan, and brought on the deadly ambush of the peaceful settlers.

Ten days after the 1791 assault took place, Jonathan Greathouse and his intended bride, Henrietta Rigby, were found on the riverbank, naked, with his entrails strung out on saplings and her body ravaged by hogs. Fortunately, this was the last recorded attack staged on flatboats on the Ohio after General Anthony Wayne subdued the Iroquois by 1794.[8]

3. Kentucky and Tennessee border states.

Subsequently, Ridgely's grandfather, George Lewis, settled in Mason County on the south side of the natural bend of the Ohio River, where he signed a petition to form the town of Washington, Kentucky, in 1786. In a few years Lewis resettled at Clarks Station, renaming it Lewis Station to provide accommodations for travelers. Lewis served as a representative to frame the Kentucky Constitution,

8. Clift, G. Glenn. *History of Maysville and Mason County, Kentucky,* Vol. 1 (Lexington: Transylvania Printing Co., 1936), pp. 103-106.

and later established Lewisburg on his 70 acres of land. This ambitious ancestor also located a farm in Christian County, in the northwestern corner of Kentucky.

Despite the potential danger, settlers like the Lewis and the Greathouse families kept coming down the river to Mason County. These pioneers found that the dangers paled in comparison to the land's potential prospects. Ridgely's father, William Greathouse, established himself in Washington, Kentucky. By 1803 the growing village had 200 wooden houses, a brisk trade in corn to New Orleans, and fine plantations with well-constructed enclosures.

The Greathouse plantation was on the outer edge of the Bluegrass Country where the labor-intensive cash crops were tobacco and hemp. Utilizing slave labor and clay from the farm, a 13-room mansion was solidly constructed, three bricks thick. Slave quarters and a stone root cellar were additions.[9] Tradition claims the barn was built from the flatboat in which the Greathouse family arrived on the Ohio River. Besides corn and wheat, plantation owners like William grew the profitable crops of hemp, tobacco, and cotton. Because efforts to hire Irish or German immigrants were unsuccessful and disappointing, the growers remained economically dependent on slave labor.

Ridgely's father, William Greathouse, served in the "Forgotten War" of 1812, when the British invaded the city of Washington, D.C., and torched it and the capitol building. Kentuckians who could have included William Greathouse were then recruited by Andrew Jackson to successfully defend the port of New Orleans, also under attack.

Later, William studied law and was admitted to the bar at Lexington, Kentucky, but he spent his life in the business of farm-

---

9. Holleran, Lucy, "Exploring Maysville and Mason County: Greathouse, great story." Lifestyle, *The Ledger Independent*, April 20, 2019. Also, Maysville-Mason County Convention Bureau, accessed March 26, 2020. CVB@VisitMaysvilleKY

ing and stock raising.[10] In 1815, he married Jane Lewis, a native of Mason County, where the ambitious Lewis family had gained considerable means. Many such gentlemen of prestige and wealth, including William Greathouse, enjoyed a good match race with thoroughbred horses. In the fall of 1827, the Maysville Jockey Club sponsored a race with 3-year-old colts, in two-mile heats. William's gray gelding, Telegraph, won the purse of $100 for his plantation owner.[11]

It was a slave auction in 1833 on the courthouse steps at Washington, Kentucky, that drew the attention of Harriet Beecher Stowe. The unforgettable, heart-wrenching scene was incorporated into her book, *Uncle Tom's Cabin*, published nearly 20 years later.

The slavery question would continue to divide the states of Ohio and Kentucky, their constituents, communities, and families. Through the Underground Railway, a network of individuals facilitated escapes or provided encouragement, shelter, and food for slaves in their attempts to obtain freedom. By just crossing the river at Maysville into Ohio in 1838, blacks could be free. John B. Mahan, an abolitionist minister from Ohio, allowed 15 slaves to pass through his farm, although it was illegal in Kentucky to assist runaways. He was therefore indicted for the abduction of slaves belonging to William Greathouse. Mahan's acquittal resulted in Mason County slave holders forming an association to address the situation. The slavery issue was also complicated by the dependence of prospering Maysville upon the plantation crops for the raw material needed for its factories, including hemp rope walks and power looms for making hemp bags, as well as industrial businesses such as flour mills, saw mills, tobacco manufacturing, wool carding, and plow manufacturing.

10. "Henry Greathouse," biographical souvenir of the state of Texas (Chicago: F.A. Battey & Co., 1889).

11. Clift, G. Glenn. *History of Maysville and Mason County, Kentucky*, Vol. 1 (Lexington: Transylvania Printing Co., 1936), p. 165.

By the 1840s, opposition to the slavery issue became stronger, yet some Kentuckians still remained neutral. Secessionists supported the institution of slavery and states' rights, but the Copperhead Democrats, sometimes known as the Peace Democrats, were opposed to both war and splitting the Union. Another faction was in favor of preserving the Union above all else, and that was personified by Lucien Greathouse, a cousin to William, who became the youngest colonel in the Union Army and laid down his life for his beliefs.[12]

Adding to the mounting war hysteria over the slavery issue, U.S. Secretary of War William Seward ordered, by President Lincoln's direction, the arrest and imprisonment of an active group of secessionists. Without fair hearing or trial, they were sent to Fort Lafayette, New York, a federal prison for political prisoners. Although the suspension of habeas corpus was forbidden by the Constitution, the clause "when in Cases of Rebellion or Invasion the public safety may require it" was applied. After intersessions were made on the prisoners' behalf, they were released by taking an oath of loyalty to the United States. This issue again would be challenged during Abraham Lincoln's administration. Finally, in 1866, with a Supreme Court ruling that "military trials in areas where the civil courts were capable of functioning were illegal," habeas corpus was restored.[13]

A protest party known as the Whigs formed to challenge the Jacksonian Democrats and address concerns of the slavery issue, the treatment of Indians, the Texas War of Independence against Mexico, German and Irish immigration, neutrality, and the emancipation of the slaves. According to Mason County historian G.

---

12. Bailey, Christopher H. *The Stulls of "Millsborough," A Genealogical History of John Stull "the Miller," Pioneer of Western Maryland*, Vol. 1 (C.H. Bailey; limited first edition, January 2000), p. 561. Also can be viewed online at https://www.familysearch.org/library/books/records/item/420731-redirection

13. "Did President Lincoln suspend Habeas Corpus?" *American Patriot Network.* http://civil-liberties.com/pages/did_lincoln.htm

Glenn Clift, "It is extremely doubtful if over the vast theatre of the Civil War a section was more cursed by division and loyalties than was Mason [County, Kentucky], borderland of every strife."

During these years of unrest and conflict, Ridgely was growing to manhood in Kentucky, tutored at home by his mother who instilled in him a love of the classics, poetry, and the finer things of life. The plantations, however, were facing economic difficulties as drought created crop failures, a scarcity of hemp seed, the loss of the tobacco cash crop, and the lack of cotton to pick. These difficulties were intensified by the tight labor situation and the growing sentiment against holding slaves. On the 1840 census, Ridgley's father, William Greathouse, reported his farm had a total of 17 slaves, which included only one person involved in agriculture, an older couple about 65 years old, seven others of working age, and nine children of varying ages. According to the slave schedule in the 1850 Federal Census, William reported one black female, age 75, one male, age 28, and four children aged 6 to 12. An 85-year-old female slave was the only one enumerated in 1860. William likely never was a big slave holder on his farm.

The future for plantations did not look good, and with the death of matriarch Jane Lewis Greathouse in 1849, it was time for a change. Rumors of easily available California gold and attendant job opportunities looked mighty enticing to several branches of the Greathouse clan. Hoping to strike it rich, William Greathouse's sons and extended family members of the Greathouse clan and Tevis clan (also extended family of the Greathouse clan) joined thousands upon thousands in the 1849 Gold Rush.

CHAPTER 3

California Beckons

The lure of adventure and the possibility of quick gain drew Ridgely's older brothers, George, 29, and Henry, 21, to California, a compromise-free state ratified in 1850 and carved from the territory recently acquired in the Mexican-American War (1846-1848.)

No description of the brothers' exodus from Kentucky was found, but a distant cousin, Robert Greathouse from Conway County, Arkansas, headed out overland with a party through Arizona Territory. Although they suffered from lack of water in their crossing, the party eventually arrived at Sacramento, California. When the mining venture did not pan out, the Arkansas cousin took a job as a gambler. In 1851, he returned home by taking a clipper ship to Panama City, a mule caravan across the Isthmus of Panama, and another clipper ship to New Orleans. From there he took a steamer up the Mississippi River to the mouth of the Arkansas River and home.[14]

To protect cross-country travelers and ensure a route for the proposed transcontinental railroad, the United States purchased 30

---

14. Greathouse, Jack Murray, "My Grandfather's Trip to California in 1849," *A Partial History of the Greathouse Family in America*, No. 7, Bulletin Series (Fayetteville, Arkansas: Washington County Historical Society, 1954), pp. 43-44.

square miles of Arizona Territory from Mexico in 1851 for $10 million. By 1858, The Overland Mail Company dipped down from St. Louis to Fort Smith, Arkansas, and then to Sherman and El Paso, Texas, to Yuma, Arizona, and north to Los Angeles and Sacramento, California. The route covered 2,600 miles in 20 punishing days and nights. A more time-consuming trail option was a four- to six-month trek, if there were no snow delays, from Independence, Missouri, along the Oregon Trail to Idaho, and then the California Trail to Sacramento, California.

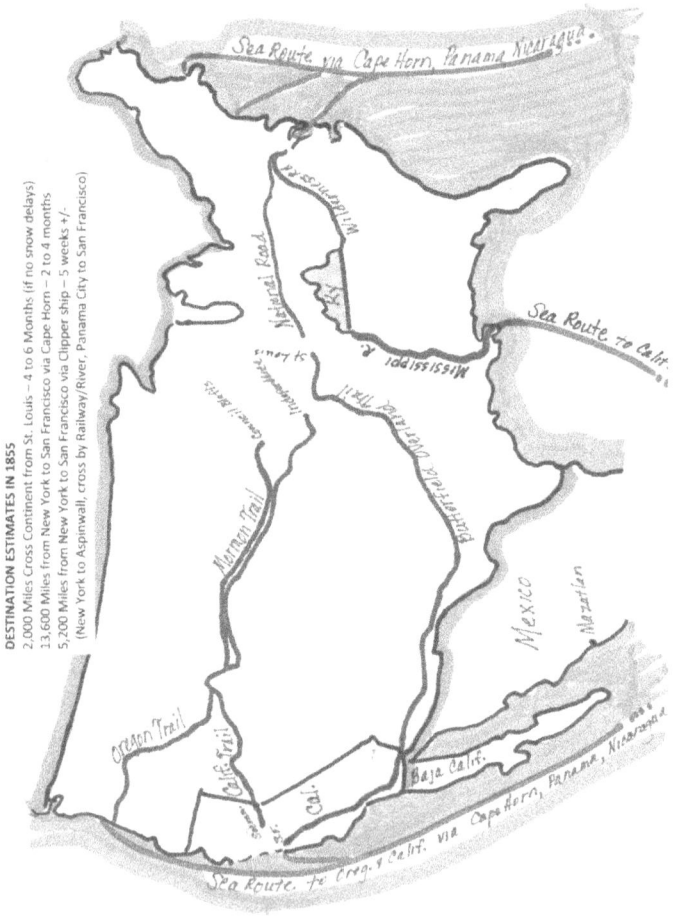

4. Gold field routes, 1855.

An alternate but popular sea route was a three-month trip from New York, around the tip of South America via Cape Horn to San Francisco. As the demand grew for better and faster transportation to the gold fields, clipper ships left New York or New Orleans for the Isthmus of Panama. There, passengers embarked on a dangerous jungle route of 47 miles by mule train and canoe, then boarded another clipper ship to San Francisco, cutting the en route time to six weeks or less from the Louisiana port. When American investment pushed the Aspinwall Railway across the Isthmus in 1855, the time was shaved down to about five weeks from New York. Each of these travel options presented its share of hazards, hardships, and dangers.

Soon after their arrival in California, George and Henry realized there were other opportunities besides gold mining available near Yreka, located in the newly formed Siskiyou County near the Oregon Territory border.

"In the summer of 1851," wrote George, "I went to Sacramento without a dollar, disgusted with the mines. Borrowed $150 of Loyd Tevis, my cousin. Bought two mules. Took them to Marysville and Downieville. Advertised to carry passengers over the road on my mules and all other matters on which people were willing to pay express prices. The first trip I made one mule clear and have been in the same business ever since."[15]

Joined by Ridgely, then 21, the Greathouse Brothers' ventures in 1852 included a partnership with Hugh Slicer in a stage and express line, a bank, and a water company to carry ditchwater over 90 miles to placer miners in the Yreka Basin. Besides serving as treasurer of the water company for his brother George who acted as president, Ridgely transported gold dust and coin, mail, and

---

15. George Lewis Greathouse correspondence to Lewis Keysor Wood. *Western Express*, March 1996. Western Cover Society, Vol. 46, No. 1.

supplies by pack train over rugged trails and led mule passenger rides over the mountains to Shasta.[16] Among the dangers he faced were robbers, hostile Indians, rockslides, snow avalanches, and treacherous river crossings.

By 1855, the youngest Greathouse brother, Robert Langhorne, then 19 years old, also resided in Shasta, California. He remained there until Henry traveled to the Texas frontier three years later, adding to the investment opportunities held in common for all of the brothers. In 1859 Henry, as an agent for R.L. and Bill Greathouse, paid taxes in Gonzales County on a ranch consisting of 176 acres and 100 head of cattle,[17] including plenty of free open-range grazing. By the 1860 slave schedules in the Federal Census, Robert Greathouse enumerated one 15-year-old black slave who became known as Bill Greathouse. Unless they were growing cotton in the northeast part of Texas or on the coastal prairie, most Texans had just a few, if any, slaves to help around the farms or ranches.

Political Intrigue

As the banking business of Greathouse & Brothers prospered, Ridgely began to spend more and more time in Sacramento and San Francisco. The prosperous California Territory drew people from around the world. With the influx came an explosive mix of Southern and Northern attitudes and cultures, creating a great amount of political intrigue in San Francisco. Fights, duels, and murders erupted over matters of opinion expressed on one side or the other.

---

16. Fullerton, George E., "The Fabulous Greathouse Brother," *Los Angeles Corral of Westerners* (Los Angeles: The Seventh Brand Book, 1957). http://www.westerners-los-angeles.org/The_Brand_Books

17. Tax rolls of 1860, Gonzales County, Texas.

In this atmosphere, Southern sympathizers, as Ridgely was, found it expedient to meet in discrete locations and through secret organizations to carry on their political discourses. Filling the bill was the Knights of the Golden Circle (KGC), organized in Kentucky in 1854 as an extension of various Southern Rights groups. Members gathered in clandestine meetings to address how they might assist the Southern cause as they took an oath to support the brotherhood upon the threat of death. Identifying signs, handshakes, and secret codes were used to communicate.

The primary goal of the KGC was to create a prosperous, slave-holding Southern empire, encompassing a circle or crescent from Cuba to the southern states of the United States, Mexico, Gulf of Mexico, Central America, and the Caribbean. Slave labor, accepted around the world at that time, would drive a thriving economy, fueled by cotton, sugarcane, tobacco, rice, coffee, indigo, and mining.[18]

Spurred by a desire to add future slave states to the Union, military filibusters encouraged revolutions in unstable countries. These freebooters, as they were known in the English press, found private sources to finance their illegal expeditions to take over the governments in Cuba, Mexico, and Central America. Whether motivated by greed, political ideology, or the thrill of adventure, filibusters found the concept of Manifest Destiny useful to their aims. Coined by John O'Sullivan in 1845, Manifest Destiny was the belief that it was the will of God that the United States should expand into and control the entire North American continent.[19]

---

18. "Knights of the Golden Circle." http://knightsofthegoldencircle.webs.com/
"K.G.C. An authentic exposition of the origin, objects, and secret work of the organization known as the Knights of the Golden Circle," University of Michigan, accessed March 10, 2012. https://quod.lib.umich.edu/m/moa/ANY1772.0001.001
19. Daniel, Clinton, Editor. *Chronicle of America* (Mount Kisco, New York: Chronicle Publications, 1989), p. 322.

The Knights of the Golden Circle, drunk with possibilities from the acquisition of the territories of California and New Mexico through the U. S. war of aggression against Mexico (1846-1847), plotted dynasties that were theirs for the taking. In this volatile political atmosphere fostered by the KGC, Ridgely, a Southerner to the core, became acquainted with Asbury Harpending, an ardent secessionist. Harpending advocated the takeover of California to create the Republic of the Pacific and planned to outfit a steamer as a privateer.[20]

At age 15, Harpending ran away from school to join a group going to the aid of William Walker in Nicaragua, but the plan unraveled and the youth returned home with his absence undetected.[21] With the intent to colonize La Paz in Mexican Baja California and lower California, Walker declared himself Nicaraguan president in 1853. Backed by Accessory Transit Shipping Lines owned by Cornelius Vanderbilt, Walker went further two years later and declared himself dictator of Nicaragua during a civil war there. When the freebooters invaded Costa Rica in 1856, however, Vanderbilt withdrew any support, cut off the shipping line of supplies, and sent his own private army to take Walker back to the U.S. as a prisoner. Although Walker escaped and returned to Central America, he was executed in Honduras, in revenge for the hundreds killed in Nicaragua during his reign of terror in his attempted coup.[22]

20. Harpending, Asbury. *The Great Diamond Hoax and other Stirring Incidents in the Life of Asbury Harpending* (San Francisco: James H. Barry Co., 1913), chapter X.

21. Gilbert, Benjamin Franklin, "Kentucky Privateers in California," *Kentucky State Historical Society*, Vol. 38. No. 124, p. 256.

22. Daniel, Clinton, Editor. *Chronicle of America* (Mount Kisco, New York: Chronicle Publications, 1989), pp. 349, 351, 354.

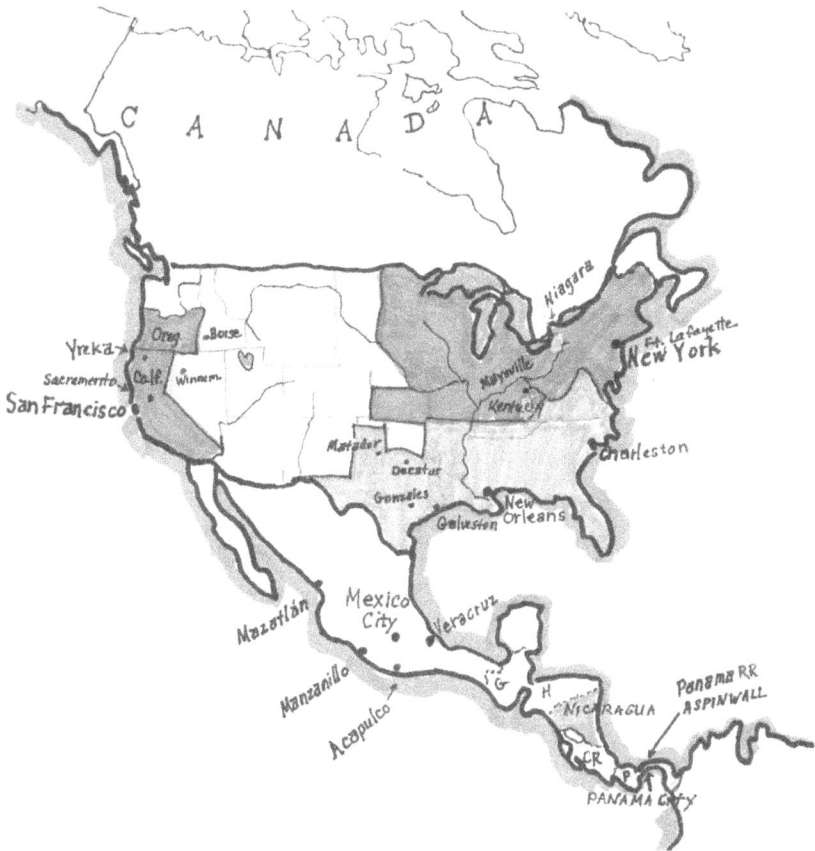

5. *United States, Mexico, and Panama routes.*

The Watermelon Riot

By design or by accident, Ridgely Greathouse, at age 25, was in Panama City on April 15, 1856. There, a California group of fili-busters from the steamship *Cortes* was detained on their way to assist William Walker but became stranded at the terminus of the Panama crossing. In addition, nearly a thousand passengers out of New York with connections to San Francisco had arrived on the eastern side at Aspinwall, Panama. Packed into the paddle-wheel steamship *Illinois*, the travelers endured extreme overcrowding, unacceptable sanitation conditions, and a shortage of food and water. After a rail-car trip across the Isthmus, the stressed passengers, some of whom had been drinking heavily, arrived at Panama City. To their dismay, they found the ferry that was scheduled to take them to the steam-ship for San Francisco was grounded by low tide and wouldn't be available until the tide returned.

Extremely disgruntled, individuals spread out along the wharf, looking for food, drink, and diversion. An American filibuster's snitch of a watermelon slice from a vendor led to retaliation—a fight that mushroomed into a native uprising. Ignited by the aggression of the stranded filibusters, the violence was stoked by native resentment of the American domination of the railway and the lack of jobs available for locals.

When the smoke cleared, 25 Americans and at least two, possibly up to 15, *Panameños* were killed. Estimations included an equal number of wounded, including Backus, the colored servant traveling with Ridgely Greathouse.[23] The survivors awaited transportation to carry them away while the U.S. Marines quelled the disturbance. About two weeks afterward, the arrival in San Francisco of Greathouse and the wounded Backus made news in both the San Francisco and Sacramento newspapers.[24] Internationally, the incident became known as "The Watermelon Riot."

23. "Arrival of the J.L. Stephens," *Sacramento Daily Union*, Vol. 11, No. 1592, May 2, 1856. https://cdnc.ucr.edu/?a=d&d=SDU18560502&e=-------en--20--1--txt-txIN--------1; "Additional Information on the Riot," *Sacramento Daily Union*, Vol. 11, No. 1594, May 5, 1856. California Digital Newspaper Collection; *Sacramento Daily Union*, accessed Jan. 30, 2012. https://cdnc.ucr.edu/?a=d&d=SDU18560505&e=-------en--20--1--txt-txIN--------1
"Watermelon Riot's Killed, Wounded, and Missing," *San Francisco Herald*, May 2, 1856, 2:1: "Full Particulars of the Riot and Massacre at Panama," May 2, 1856. GenealogyBank.
24. Marilou West Ficklin, "The Watermelon Riot, Panama 1856" c. 2004. "The Panama Massacre – The Watermelon Riot," c. 2006, accessed Nov. 17, 2011. http://www.westerly-journeys.com/goldrush/goldpanama.html

U.S. President Pierce later issued a proclamation that all private damage claims of passengers and companies would be evaluated by a claims convention. Never one to miss an opportunity, Greathouse's claim stated that "he is a citizen of the United States, that he was in Panama, on the 15th of April 1856 during the riot—that he had to flee from the house in which he was, to save his life—leaving behind his baggage which he has never recovered, that the value of said Baggage was One Hundred and Thirty Dollars." Ridgely, as his name was recorded by a notary on the 1st of April, 1861, authorized his attorney to collect and receive the $130 for the damage to his luggage,[25] but none was asked or received for the injury to his servant in the infamous Watermelon Riot.

---

25. Ridgely Greathouse, Claim No. 101, on page 282 of Consular Letters, January to July 1856, and notarized copy authorizing John Bryant, Attorney, to operate on his behalf. https://law.resource.org/pub/reporter/F.cas10026.f.cas.0018.2.pdf
Claim No. 101, Ridgely Greathouse: Columbia Conventions of 1857 and 1864. Docketed Cases, 1861-62 and 1865-66; Entry Pl 177 75; Records of Boundary and Claims Commissions and Arbitrations, Record Group 76. The seven pages of copies from the National Archives were received in December 2011 by Danella Reno Dickson.
Additional research notes: The story of the Watermelon Riot was published in newspapers at that time and retold in articles by Marilou West Ficklin: "The Watermelon Riot—Details," published in *Western Journeys*, 2006. http://www.westerly-journeys.com/gold-rush/goldriot-details.html

CHAPTER 4

Storm Clouds on the Horizon

While Ridgely's brothers Henry and Robert Langhorne Greathouse were involved in the family ranching endeavor in Texas, Ridgely joined his brother George in banking and other ventures, including the express line to deliver mail. The stage line partnership with Hugh Slicer in Yreka, California, dissolved in 1857. The following year, the brothers were awarded the mail contracts from Crescent City on the California coast to Jacksonville, 90 miles and back, once a week, with George receiving $2,970 and Ridgely, $2,370.[26]

During the years of 1859 and 1860, Ridgely served as treasurer for the town of Yreka. As the new mountain pass road for passengers and freighting was improved by a turnpike company, Greathouse & Company became the first line of through-stages from Yreka to Red Bluff. When heavy floods swept away their bridges and roads, the company was out of business, and so were George and his brother/partner Ridgely, who looked for new opportunities in Sacramento and San Francisco.

---

26. "Contracts for Carrying the Mails, Route No. 12558." George L. Greathouse and Ridgely Greathouse. 1859-03-01. http://www.genealogybank.com/gbnk/documents/doc/v2%3A0FD2A62D41CEB699%40GBDOC

6. Knights of the Golden Circle.

As the storm clouds of war gathered over the nation in 1860, The Knights of the Golden Circle (KGC) held their convention in Raleigh, North Carolina. Their records claimed a large membership in the North that supported the constitutional rights of the South, as well as a ready army of around 14,000, with new recruits joining daily.[27] A plan for the invasion of Mexico along the Rio Grande had faltered. A second plan was forgotten when the election of Abraham Lincoln prompted the secession movement and took center stage. On December 20, 1860, South Carolina voted to secede from the Union, followed in 1861 by the states of Mississippi, Florida, Alabama, Georgia, and Louisiana.

---

27. Knights of the Golden Circle. https://knightsofthegoldencircle.webs.com/

In anticipation of what was to come, Texas volunteer forces under the command of Colonel Ben McCulloch forced the surrender of the federal arsenal in San Antonio on February 23, 1861. Among their ranks were 150 members of KGC, including Captain Trevanion Teel, Sergeant R.G. Williams, Sergeant Morgan Wolfe Merrick, and John Robert Baylor. Other KGC companies forced the surrender of federal posts from San Antonio to El Paso.[28]

Call for Privateers

The Confederate States of America had almost no navy, so the provisional president of the Confederacy, Jefferson Davis, issued a proclamation offering to give official sanction, known as a *letter of marque*, to any armed private vessel that was willing to attack Northern ships.[29] With the issue of letters of marque, privateering and reprisal, the forceable seizure of an enemy's goods or subjects were practices explicitly allowed by the Confederate Constitution, as well as the United States Constitution from which they were copied. The privateers were expected to prey on commercial vessels of the enemy, which would then be sold. The profits, less expenses, would be turned over to the Confederacy, the United States, or other warring nations' governments. Many ship owners, as well as pirates, responded to the appeal by applying for letters of marque to the government they represented.

Ridgely's KGC acquaintance, Asbury Harpending, decided to answer the call. Aside from his Southern patriotism, financial benefit was an obvious incentive. The Confederate law was sufficiently liberal

---

28. Knights of the Golden Circle. https://knightsofthegoldencircle.webs.com/

29. Proclamation by Jefferson Davis. www.newsinhistory.com/blog/confederate-president-davis-encourages-privateers

to consider privateering as an institution of gain.[30] The Republic of the Pacific plot for takeover of California had fizzled by this time. Backing Harpending in a new scheme were several prominent men, including Ridgely Greathouse. They were willing to pledge $250,000 to disrupt or seize on the high seas the Pacific Mail gold shipments essential to the U.S. government in Washington, D.C.[31]

Since Harpending claimed he had no stomach for piracy, he was determined to receive a regular commission from the Confederate Navy to legitimize their efforts. To avoid detection, he took a steamship to Acapulco, then rode horseback across Mexico, and by his account, was waylaid by bandits on the way to Mexico City. He continued without further incident to Vera Cruz where he boarded a Confederate blockade runner and slipped past federal warships to Charleston. From there he went to Richmond, Virginia, to confer with the president of the Confederacy, Jefferson Davis.[32]

President Davis warned Harpending about the dangers of piracy, but through Judah Benjamin, a cabinet member, offered a plan that would legitimize the endeavor under international law. A commander would outfit a vessel in any U.S. port, travel to a foreign port, exhibit letters of marque and, before any engagement, declare the purpose of preying on U.S. commerce. According to Harpending, Davis sent him off with a *blank* letter of marque[33] to

---

30. Robinson, William Morrison, Jr. *The Confederate Privateers* (Columbia, South Carolina: University of South Carolina Press, 1990), pp. 21, 23.

31. Harpending, Asbury. *The Great Diamond Hoax and other Stirring Incidents in the Life of Asbury Harpending* (San Francisco: The James H. Barry Co., 1913), chapter VI, p. 1. Online reproduction can be found at http://www.books-about-california.com/Pages/The_Great_Diamond_Hoax/

32. Ibid.

33. Robinson, William Morrison, Jr. *The Confederate Privateers* (Columbia, South Carolina: University of South Carolina Press, 1990), pp 17, 20. Harpending's veracity about receiv-

be filled out in a foreign port, with instructions to implement it and correspond to certain Southern supporters.[34] On his return trip, Harpending abandoned the Mexican route and went through Panama, arriving in California in July 1862.

The privateering plans to purchase a fast-sailing schooner were proceeding when the 90-ton *Chapman* arrived in San Francisco from New York. A young Englishman, Albert Rubery, who was a friend of Harpending and a Southern sympathizer, offered to purchase the craft with a bank draft, but his funds proved insufficient. Harpending, supposedly rich from gold mining, was for the moment financially embarrassed, having expended "nearly every cent he had" to obtain the letter of marque. Greathouse stepped in with the capital to finance the scheme, thereby assuming the title of "Captain Greathouse."[35] He purchased the schooner for $6,500 and paid for arms, munitions, uniforms, and supplies, as well as the hire of a mate and crew of 15.[36]

---

ing a blank letter of marque is questioned by the third and fourth sections contained in "An Act recognizing the existence of war between the United States and the Confederate States; and concerning letters of marque, prizes, and prize goods." It stated that the applicant must own a specific ship and that no commission could be issued in blank, nor would a transfer of flag from one ship to another be tolerated.

34. Harpending, Asbury. *The Great Diamond Hoax and Other Stirring Incidents in the Life of Asbury Harpending* (San Francisco: The James H. Barry Co., 1913), chapter VI, p. 45. See Appendix A for list of crew members. Online reproduction can be found at http://www.books-about-california.com/Pages/The_Great_Diamond_Hoax/

35. "The Chapman Case," *Sacramento Daily Union*, Vol. 26, Number 3914, October 9, 1863. GenealogyBank.

36. Gilbert, Benjamin Franklin, "Kentucky Privateers in California," *Kentucky State Historical Society*, Vol. 38. No. 124, pp. 256-266.

7. Schooner similar to the J.M. Chapman. *Art by Kayla White.*

The trio—Greathouse, Harpending, and Rubery—proposed to sail the schooner to the small island of Guadalupe, Mexico, and outfit it into a fighting craft to waylay the Pacific Mail steamers. Then they would port in Manzanillo where they would write their names in the blank letter of marque and forward it to the Confederate capital, thereby legitimizing their privateering plunder. All that was missing was a navigator. Southern gentlemen, after all, had few opportunities in piloting schooners. A navigator was found in William Law, but his loyalty was questionable from the start. When it was time to sail on the evening of March 14, 1863, Law did not appear, nor did he the next morning because he had spilled the scheme to law enforcement.

Determined to get underway at dawn, "Captain" Greathouse ordered Seaman Libby to hoist the sails in San Francisco Bay, only to find the *Chapman* blocked by the guns of the *U.S. Crane*. As authorities boarded the *Chapman*, Harpending and Rubery tried to destroy incriminating papers but were thwarted in their efforts to either shred or eat them. Abstracts from the *Sacramento Union* newspaper of March 15, 1863, summarized the situation: "Schooner *J.M. Chapman*, fitted out for a piratical cruise in the Pacific, was seized at San Francisco by the federal authorities. The ring leaders were imprisoned at Alcatraz and placed in irons, and the others were also detained on the island."[37]

37. "Noticeable Events During the Year," *The Sacramento Union*, January 1, 1864, p. 1. GenealogyBank. http://www.NewspaperAbstract.com

CHAPTER 5

Indictment and Trial

After a few days of confinement, Greathouse was released on bail furnished by his cousin, Loyd Tevis, a successful lawyer turned banker and capitalist.[38] That left the co-conspirators in prison, a situation that did not go unnoticed by the detainees. Harpending later related that the freed Greathouse visited them at the Old Broadway Jail where they'd been transferred. Greathouse was in great spirits and full of a good lunch. He allowed that the prospects for the others weren't that promising, "I guess we'll all have to go to prison for a while, but I'll be able to buy my way out."[39]

That foolish talk, according to Harpending, prompted Libby, a Canadian without friends or funds, to turn state's evidence. The indictment that resulted, *United States v. Greathouse et al., 1863,*

---

38. Loyd Tevis's mother was Sarah Greathouse, sister to Ridgely's father William. Tevis owned controlling interest in Wells Fargo & Co. in 1869 and served as president of the company from 1872 to 1892. Besides stage lines, he was involved in street cars, mining, telegraph, ranching, land promotion, and ice, gas and express companies.

39. Harpending, Asbury. *The Great Diamond Hoax and Other Stirring Incidents in the Life of Asbury Harpending* (San Francisco: The James H. Barry Co., 1913), chapter VI, p. 45. Online reproduction can be found at http://www.books-about-california.com/Pages/The_Great_Diamond_Hoax/

alleged in substance: (1) The existence of a rebellion against the United States, their authority, and laws; (2) That the defendants traitorously engaged in, and gave aid and comfort to, the same; (3) That in the execution of their treasonable purposes, they procured, fitted out, and armed a vessel to cruise in the service of the rebellion on the high seas, and commit hostilities against the citizens, property, and vessels of the United States, and that vessel sailed on such a cruise.[40]

Ridgely Greathouse, Asbury Harpending, and Alfred Rubery were tried in the Federal District Court of the Northern District of California. Their counsel argued that the schooner had not commenced her cruise and no offense had been committed. "There could be no treason and no conviction under the indictment for the reason that 'aid and comfort' had not been actually given."[41]

After several weeks of testimonies, however, a jury deliberation of only four minutes convicted the three of treason. John Bright of England petitioned President Lincoln to pardon Alfred Rubery, and as a favor to their friendship and as ally of the U.S., the president issued the General Amnesty Act of December 8, 1863. Judge Ogden Hoffman notified Lincoln that the language was too broad in legal terms and needed to be clarified with another document. With no clarification from Lincoln, Judge Hoffman's liberal and controversial interpretation allowed Greathouse to take an oath of allegiance

---

40. *United States v. Greathouse et al.* 2 Abb. U.S. 364, 4 Sawy.457,26F. Cas. 18, No. 15,254, Oct. 17, 1863. https://law.resource.org/pub/us/case/reporter/F.Cas/0026.f.cas/0 026.f.cas.0018.2.pdf

41. *United States v. Greathouse et al.*, 21-22. The Federal Cases: Comprising Cases Argued Determined in the Circuit and District Courts of the U.S., Bk. XXVI, Case No. 15,254, 8-30, St. Paul, 1894-1898.

to the U.S. and become a free man. Harpending refused to take the oath and remained in jail.[42]

Four months into the sentence of 10 years' imprisonment, Judge Hoffman also ordered Harpending's release under the General Amnesty Act and cancellation of the $10,000 fine. The prisoner walked from prison a free man, but friends of Harpending feared the government might change its mind and took up a collection, urging him to flee. He headed toward Santa Cruz, California, but was advised to hide out in an obscure mining town near Kernville. His time was well rewarded in the mining region. Through hard work and perseverance, by his count he eventually tallied up to $800,000[43] in gold, mine claims, and stock in his career of fortunes lost and fortunes gained.

The Tide Turns

Greathouse, on the other hand, found the tide had turned on his good fortune. On April 7, 1864, by the order of Secretary of War Edwin Stanton to Brigadier General George Wright, Ridgely was seized on the streets of Yreka and arrested as a "dangerous criminal." The charges against him stemmed back to a series of loyalty oaths he took in order to travel back to his family home in the Union-held state of Kentucky. His father, William, had passed away sometime later in 1863. For whatever personal or political reasons that he had for traveling to Kentucky, Ridgely violated his parole and his oaths

---

42. Gilbert, Benjamin Franklin, "Kentucky Privateers in California," *Kentucky State Historical Society*, Vol. 38. No. 124, pp. 256-266.

43. Harpending, Asbury. *The Great Diamond Hoax and Other Stirring Incidents in the Life of Asbury Harpending* (San Francisco: The James H. Barry Co., 1913), chapter VI, p. 48. Online reproduction can be found at http://www.books-about-california.com/Pages/The_Great_Diamond_Hoax/

of loyalty to the United States by planning to aid the Confederacy, opening himself up to the charge of treason and punishment of death as provided by the military code.

One of three passes, found in his personal trunk at the first arrest, granted permission to pass beyond St. Louis, Missouri, to Louisville, Kentucky. Issued to R. Greathouse, age 28, blue eyes, light-colored hair, on September 4, 1861, it stated: "*It is understood that the within named and subscriber accepts this pass on his word of honor that he is and will be ever loyal to the United States: and if hereafter found in arms against the Union, or in any way aiding her enemies, the penalty will be death.*"

A second pass stated the following: /No. 253/ Military pass, Headquarters Dep't of Ohio, Louisville (KY) Feb. 5, 1862, Pass Bearer, Mr. R. Greathouse through our lines to Evansville, by command of Brig. General Buel, A.F. Rochmond, Aide-de-Camp. "*I solemnly swear without any mental reservation or evasion, that I will support the Constitution of the United States and the laws made pursuance thereof: that I will not take up arms against the United States, or give aid of comfort or furnish information directly or indirectly to any person or persons belonging to any of the so-styled Confederate States, who are now, or may be, in rebellion against the Government of the United States, so help me God. It is understood that the penalty for the violation of this pass is death. Ridgely Greathouse.*"

The third pass in question stated: "*Permit of Provost Marshall. By order of the Commanding General, Ridgely Greathouse is allowed to pass from Evansville to Henderson, Kentucky, on the river, he having taken the oath to support the Constitution of the United States and be true and loyal to the United States and the State of Indiana, and that he will not divulge or reveal anything he may see or hear within our lines, or give aid or comfort to our enemies.*

Blythe Hynes, Provost Marshall. Evansville (Ind) Feb. 6, 1862."
On the back was a description of his person: Ridgely Greathouse,
age 30, 5 feet 8 inches, blue eyes, light-colored hair, light goatee
and mustache.[44]

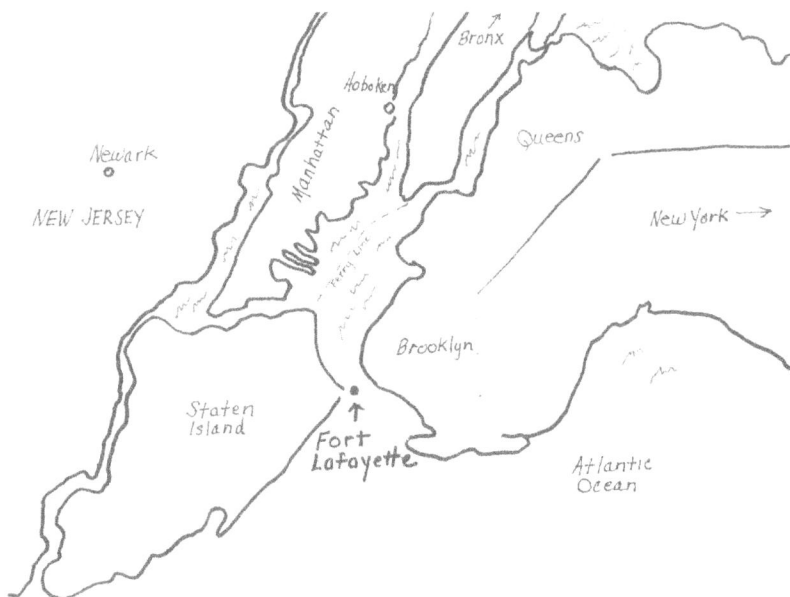

8. Fort Lafayette location.

Not for his pirating plot but for violating his oaths of loyalty to
the United States during wartime, Ridgely was re-arrested and taken
into custody in a surprise sweep on the streets of his hometown. He
was placed in heavy irons as ordered by Secretary of War Stanton to
await a military trial for treason against the United States. A week
later, the prisoner and his armed guard, destined for the fortress
prison of Fort Lafayette in New York Harbor, were aboard the
steamer *Golden City* bound for Panama, along with 350 passengers.

---

44. *Sacramento Daily Union*, Vol. 27, Number 4071, April 8, 1864; Number 4072, April
9, 1864; and Number 4074, 11 April 1864. GenealogyBank.

Ironically, $1,064,000 in treasure was also being transported under heightened alert, because just days before on April 9, 1864, the *Golden City* had been the subject of a street rumor that it had been pirated by the *Alabama*.[45]

After a trip through Panama and transfer to another steamship, Greathouse arrived at Fort Hamilton, opposite Fort Lafayette, between the lower end of Staten Island and Long Island. Like other federal political prisoners and prisoners of war en route to the offshore prison fortress, he was searched and his name recorded. Then he was placed on a boat for the quarter-mile trip to the octagonal structure built on a small rock island. There he saw a fort with walls 25 to 30 feet high and batteries of heavy artillery commanding a view of the channel. Two tiers of heavy guns and lighter barbette guns stood guard.

The commander, Lt. Charles O. Wood, was described by many of the prisoners as "brutal." Once again, the prisoners were searched, most had their money confiscated, and then they were confined in the fort's two principal gun batteries, housing up to 35 prisoners. Four casemates of the lower story had also been converted into prison rooms, eight feet high and 24 x 14 feet wide, each housing up to 30 prisoners. Dark, damp, and cold most of the time, the cells' light and heat were provided by a few candles, fireplaces, and stoves. Only a few beds were provided. Besides crowded conditions, the food tasted bad and was often served half-cooked, and the water was foul.[46] Dire though the circumstances were, Ridgely Greathouse was not to be underestimated. He started making plans to escape.

45. *Sacramento Daily Union*, Vol. 27, Number 4072, April 9, 1864 and April 11, 1864.

46. Speer, Lonnie R., *Portals to Hell: Military Prisons of the Civil War* (Mechanicsburg, Pennsylvania: Stackpole Books, 1997), accessed Jan. 24, 2012. http://www.correctionhistory.org/html/chronic/cw_pows/html/cwpows3.html

9. Federal prison, Fort Lafayette, New York. Art by Kayla White.

CHAPTER 6

California War Hysteria
to Idaho Frontier

The "Chapman Affair" set off a war hysteria in California, with people fearing an invasion or unfriendly takeover of the Territory. After Confederates fired on Fort Sumter on May 29,1861, hysteria was replaced by anger against those supporting the South. The Reverend Thomas Starr wrote from Yreka that Kentucky native George Greathouse was a strong secessionist and slave owner of a free slave.[47] Referring to the status of Backus, the servant who traveled with Ridge during the Watermelon Riot, George retorted with, "I have brought our faithful boy, Bacchus, out." Even as an adult, the freed former slave was still with George in 1864. Perhaps another slave was brought out from William Greathouse's failing farm, since on the 1860-65 tax roll for Gonzales County, Texas, R. L. Greathouse reported a 15-year-old black slave. Later identified as Bill Greathouse on the 1900 census, he was born in Kentucky but was then living in Gonzales County on a ranch of 315 acres with a free-ranging cattle herd of 800.[48]

---

47. Chandler, Robert J., "Success to Civil War Tragedy, The Greathouse Brothers of Greathouse & Slicer's Express," *Western Express Research Journal of Early Western Mails*, Vol. 46, No. 1, March 1996, p. 9.

48. Gonzales, Texas 1860 tax assessment, Real and Personal Property, Robert Greathouse, Vol. 1.

Continuing to be unrepentant in his politics or support of his brother Ridgely, George referred to his own 2-year-old son, also named Ridgley, by saying, "Ask him what he *is* and he says, 'I am a Rebel. My father is a Democrat.'" The Yreka postmaster, described by George as an abolitionist spy, continued to open his letters,[49] communications that often found their way into the newspapers. Amid the scandal of the piracy trial, the unpopular ruling by Judge Hoffman to free Ridge, and their brother's subsequent re-arrest in Yreka, the political climate intensified against the Greathouses. After a disastrous flood on the stage roads shut down their Express Company, the Greathouse family felt compelled to find new opportunities. George summed up his situation in a letter to a cousin: "I sold my Ditch [water canal] and am nearly sold out of the county, with a view of locating permanently somewhere." Ridge headed for relatives in Kentucky where he would cross Union lines three times and take an oath to be loyal upon the penalty of death. Henry looked to new stage-coaching opportunities in the emerging mining towns of eastern Oregon and Idaho, where politics took a back seat to treasure hunting.

The kind of toughness and resourcefulness the Greathouse brothers exhibited throughout their lives served Henry well in the winter of 1862. The stage-coaching brother Henry took a mule train over the torturous mountain road from Yreka to The Dalles, Oregon's jumping off place for miners, pioneers, and adventurers. Henry and his party of eight were snowed in and lost for 17 days. With nothing to eat in the last four days, the frostbitten and famished travelers finally stumbled into the Evans Ranch in Butte Creek

---

49. Chandler, Robert J., "The Greathouse Brothers & Slicer's Express," *Western Express, Research Journal of Early Western Mails*, Vol. 46, No. 1, March 1996, p. 12. Western Cover Society, 1996.

Valley. Despite their near-death experiences, Henry fearlessly turned his coaches east to the Idaho gold and silver mines, providing the best service and the fastest times through the worst country.

10. Mid-nineteenth century stagecoach. Art by Kayla White.

Beckoning the brave, the foolish, or the desperate, Idaho became the new frontier as the Shoshones attempted to defend their territory against the latest invaders. Ten mining towns supported 20,000 people in 1863. The frontier trading post of Walla Walla, Washington, provided supplies which were transported over roads, rough and mountainous, in a country sparsely timbered. A frenzy born of greed gripped the 2,500 miners who were intent on new diggings, as Henry Greathouse entered, bringing with him 230 folks from Siskiyou County, California. The challenge was getting supplies in for the winter over narrow roads. In addition, "the danger from

Indians and banditti greatly discouraged stage owners and express men. The Indians stole the horses of the stage companies. Highway men, both white and red, robbed the express messengers."[50]

By 1864, George had left the dust of California behind to join Henry's stagecoaching business in Idaho. Greathouse & Company was a major operator, carrying Wells Fargo & Company's express on daily runs between Boise and Wallula and from Placerville to Idaho City. The coaching business, even if a monopoly, had its delays. In February, heavy snow fell so deeply that six horses could not pull through an empty sled. Undeterred, Henry built a stage road from Centerville each way to Placerville and Idaho City. With the founding of a new state in mining country, a majority of the population leaned toward "the union-threatening democracy of the southwestern states."[51] Ridgely's brother Henry was too busy or too smart to get into politics, but his oldest brother George sought a new direction and served as a delegate to Henry Clay's Whig party, before it disintegrated over the slavery issue.

50. Bancroft, Hubert H. *Early Settlement of Idaho*, Bancroft Works, Vol. 31; Bancroft, Hubert H. *History of Washington, Idaho, and Montana, 1845-1889* (San Francisco: The History Co. Publishers, 1890). http://www.accessgeneaology.com/idaho/early_settlement_of_idaho.htm

51. Ibid., *Early Settlement of Idaho*.

STAGE COACHING ROUTES SERVED BY
THE GREATHOUSE BROTHERS

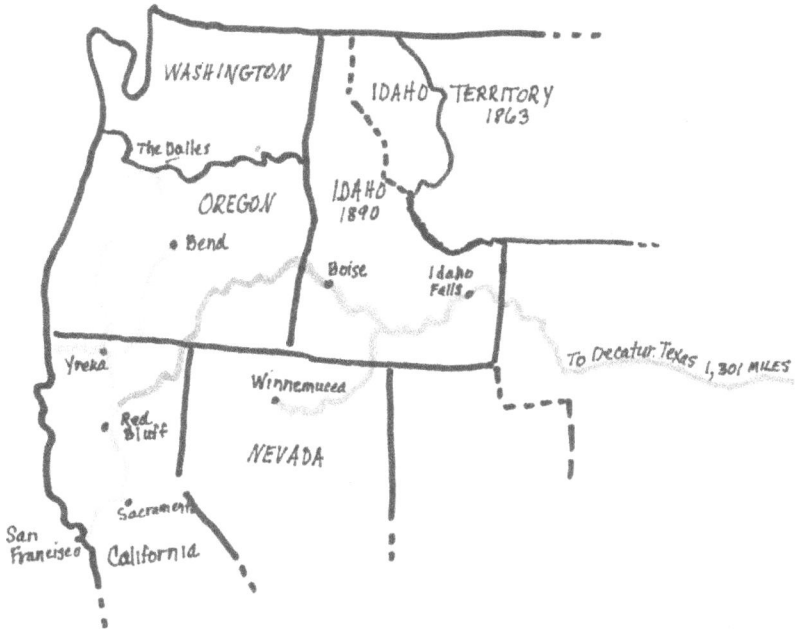

11. Stagecoach routes.

CHAPTER 7

Impossible Escape

The years spent in transporting gold dust and gold coin through the perilous California mountain passes from Red Bluff to Shasta and San Francisco perfected in Ridgely a fearlessness and heightened cunning in dangerous situations. Often alone, he encountered road agents, robbers, and hostile Indians intent on stealing the treasure from his overladen mule train. With daring and determination, he pushed through, safe and unharmed, making what were considered at the time to be near miraculous escapes.

James O'Meara, a journalist and a member of the Greathouse family by marriage, interviewed "Ridge" in 1868 in Idaho, providing a detailed account of the prisoner's escape attempt.[52] An earlier account that Ridge gave in a letter to his sister was printed in the California newspapers as breaking news: the latest on the convicted pirate. Both versions coincide, but the inquisitive newspaper man noted that Ridge seemed deeply affected by the experience, as O'Meara probed deeper for details.

---

52. O'Meara, James. "A Notable Escape," *The Californian*, Vol. 28, April 1882, pp. 341-347, accessed April 16, 2020. California State Library/LSTA Grant.

Three months in solitary confinement at Fort Lafayette gave Greathouse plenty of time to create a plan of action, but with no access to accomplices to bribe with the gold coin he collected before being arrested in Yreka. For some reason, the policy to confiscate all prisoners' money was not applied when he arrived, a fortuitous situation that was sometimes allowed for prisoners with connections or families of high standing.[53] When the cold and dank conditions took a toll on Ridgely's health, the prison's Commander Burke feared the loss of one of his prized prisoners of war. The POW had yet to stand before a court martial for treason, whereby a guilty verdict compelled a sentence of death. Should he die before the court martial, justice could not be served.

Upon the prison surgeon's recommendation, the sickly Greathouse was allowed exercise along the parapet wall and a move to a more comfortable casemate cell. There he shared quarters with a Confederate named Glassell, a man who had connections in the prison underground that offered certain benefits to those confined. A man named Allen, a New York bounty-jumper, was such a connection. He was allowed monthly visits from his wife, Mrs. Allen, who acted as a go-between with a prison broker who claimed to have influence in Washington. For $300, it was proposed, Greathouse could obtain a release, so Ridge gave her gold coins to be exchanged for currency to pay the broker. When nothing happened, Greathouse felt he had been swindled, but she continued to visit and make an exchange for greenbacks until he had exhausted the stash of $1,200 in gold coin.

---

53. In his letter to his family, Ridgely Greathouse said he was searched with his money confiscated, but in his interview with James O'Meara, he said he was allowed to keep his money.

Undeterred by the setback, Ridgely began to implement a plan. Because of the chilling weather, he had no trouble convincing Commander Burke that he needed a flannel suit and a silk cap to be secured from New York City. No longer subject to searches, Mrs. Allen gradually smuggled in several key items for his plan: a silk cord strong enough to let him down from the wall into the water, a small saw to cut his irons, and the all-important tide tables and charts of the shoreline. Likewise, he procured a bottle of brandy that could ward off the chill of the waters surrounding the island fort.

Choosing a night in the dark of the moon, he calculated the flood tide would set in just before midnight. In the meantime, he feigned exhaustion to the surgeon and Captain Burke so effectively that the guard was ordered to carry the sick man out to the fresh air of the open casemate and to leave him there for the night. This seem-ing miracle, a turn in his luck, spurred Ridge into action around 11 o'clock. He wrapped his coat and pants under his flannel suit and donned his silk cap, insulated with padded greenbacks. He crept stealthily toward the guard who had promised assistance. A sudden movement betrayed the guard's intent for betrayal.

"It was the critical moment of success or defeat, of life or death, as he felt it," O'Meara reported in the *Western Express Journal*.[54] With all his might, Greathouse related to O'Meara, he pushed the guard off the wall and into the water far below. Going around to a point jutting out from the wall, Greathouse plunged headfirst into the water. Already a strong swimmer, he was pumped up with the desperation of the moment. As he floated with the intent to sink instead of being recaptured, he watched the glare of rockets, the

---

54. O'Meara, James. "A Notable Escape," *The Californian*, Vol. 28, April 1882, p. 345, accessed April 16, 2020. California State Library/LSTA Grant.

bright lights, the flare of gunshots, and saw the oar-driven boats come close. After what seemed to be hours, all was quiet. By swimming and floating, and taking nips of the warming brandy cradled in his flannel, he reached the shoreline about daybreak.

Lieutenant Colonel Martin Burke reported a different story to his superior officers. "I cannot imagine by what means or assistance he managed to get off unless the sentinel of post was tampered with by offering a large amount of money, which the prisoner no doubt had at his command somewhere . . . The fact of this man's escape is miraculous, the guard and means adopted for the safe keeping of the prisoners at this post are ample, and I have no doubt but the sentinel on post aided and allowed the prisoner to escape in open daylight as he was reported present at Reveille this morning and not missed until 7 a.m. breakfast time."[55]

Wasting no time when he came ashore, Ridgely walked through the suburbs of Brooklyn and took a ferry to New York. He found a cheap boarding house and a second-hand store to exchange his tell-tale clothing. Later he viewed posters offering a heavy reward for his capture. After hanging out for a few days, he persuaded some boys to row him to Hoboken and bought them beer in return. From there he hiked to Newark, where he caught the night train for Philadelphia, then Pittsburg. Always friendly and charming, he daringly approached a group of soldiers and spoke to one of the officers about enlisting. At Cleveland, Ohio, he shipped out as a deckhand on a steamer going to Detroit. From his circuitous and deceiving route, he crossed over to Windsor, Canada, without difficulty.

---

55. Greathouse, Union Citizens File, B141 July 1864, Headquarters. Fold 3, p. 1.

Ridge's Escape to Canada
1. Fort Lafayette Federal Prison
2. New York, New York
3. Newark, New Jersey
4. Philadelphia, Pennsylvania
5. Pittsburg, Pennsylvania
6. Cleveland, Ohio
7. Detroit, Michigan
8. Ontario-on-the-Lake, Canada

12. Escape route to Canada.

Niagara-on-the-Lake

For two months, Ridgely remained in Niagara,[56] on the Canadian side, communicating with his family in California where the information about his successful escape was leaked to the press, perhaps by the postal employee that George Greathouse complained routinely opened his mail. The *Sacramento Daily Union* reported on April 18, 1864, "Among convicted Rebels in Niagara was Ridgeley Greathouse, freebooter."[57]

During and after the War Between the States, Ridgely and other refugee Confederates found a warm welcome at Niagara-on-the-Lake in Ontario, Canada. The loyalist settlers there shared a common bond with the Rebels, forged by a shared hostility and the Canadian loyalists' resistance to the rebellion of the United States against the mother country, England.[58] Located on a high bank overlooking the Falls, the small tourist town faced the Union's fluttering Stars and Stripes of Fort Niagara. The small community was a respite for those leaving the turmoil and mayhem of a coming war, ironically, whether they were runaway slaves who had settled there or Confederates plotting to take back their homelands held by the Union.

Once the outcome of the war seemed imminent, many Southerners, and Southern sympathizers in the North, evaded possible retribution of prison or execution for their civil and military rebellion. Fleeing the victorious Union, thousands relocated in Canada, Mexico, England, Brazil, and other countries. In the post-war years, Niagara-on-the-Lake welcomed, to mention a few, Jubal Early, John Bell Hood, James Mason, John C. Breckinridge, and Jefferson Davis,[59] the former president of the Confederacy.

---

56. Chandler, Robert J., "Success to Civil War Tragedy," p. 11, and "The Greathouse Brothers of Greathouse & Slicer's Express," *Western Express*, March 1996, p. 11.

57. *Sacramento Daily Union*, April 18, 1864.

58. Rescher, Nicholas. *Niagara-on-the-Lake as a Confederate Refuge 1866-1869* (Fox Chapel, Pennsylvania: NAP Publications, 2003), p. 9.

59. Ibid., pp. 7, 9.

When he was released on bail on May 14, 1867, Davis first visited his family in refuge at Toronto and then visited briefly with the Southerners in Niagara. Anxiety and his two years' imprisonment at Fort Monroe, Virginia, had taken its toll on Davis. His trial for treason, with execution as a possible outcome, had been postponed several times on technicalities.

Meanwhile, Constitution law experts argued that the states had a right to withdraw from the contract and had stated their reasons for secession and therefore, the reasoning proposed, the North was the aggressor.[60] After U.S. President Andrew Johnson issued his Christmas Amnesty Proclamation of 1868 to include senior officers, most of the Confederate officials, military officers, and ministers returned to their ravaged states and homes. They would resume their lives under the flag against which they had rebelled and deal with the consequences of Reconstruction retaliation.

Among the exiles leaving Canada for Europe were Jefferson Davis, John Breckinridge, and Ridgely Greathouse. After landing in Scotland, Greathouse journeyed to England where in November of 1864, he was a guest of Albert Rubery for several months. Leaving his former co-conspirator, Ridgely's destination was Mexico, a country already in turmoil from an invasion and attempted takeover by France. By order of Napoleon III, France had installed the Austrian Archduke Maximilian as Emperor of Mexico. A burgeoning exodus of Confederate soldiers considered how and where they might fit as the French army took on Benito Juarez's ill-trained and poorly equipped Juaristas in Northern Mexico.

---

60. "The Treason Trial of Jefferson Davis," Panel Discussion at the 13th Annual Elizabeth Roller Bottimore Lecture. The Museum of the Confederacy Online, accessed Dec. 3, 2011. http://www.moc.org/site/MessageViewer?em-id=4041.0

CHAPTER 8

Exiles Pour Into Mexico

The whereabouts of certain California Rebels was a hot topic in San Francisco, as the *Daily Evening Bulletin* reported on August 31, 1865: "Large numbers of disbanded soldiers of the late Confederacy are pouring into Northern Mexico. General David S. Terry, with a train including his own and several families, have arrived in Sonora by the way of Chihuahua. Col. Dan Showalter, Col. Kennedy, Ridgely Greathouse, Duncan Beaumont, and hundreds of others are at Mazatlán, and several thousands in all are scattered through these northern departments."[61]

The hegira, a mass exodus estimated to be between 5,000 and 20,000 Confederates, was motivated by other emotions in addition to fear. The possibilities for reprisals for participation in the rebellion against the United States ranged from confiscation of property to imprisonment or hanging. Conspiring to overthrow the government could bring a fine of $500 to $5,000 and the possibility of six years in prison. Treasonable activity could bring a sentence of death or five years in prison and a $10,000 fine.

---

61. "The Latest Gwin Story—Whereabouts of Certain California Rebels," *San Francisco Daily Evening Bulletin*, August 31, 1865, Issue 124; *San Francisco Examiner*, August 30, 1865. https://www.newspapers.com/

While the initial amnesty offered hope, it was so restrictive that 150,000 Southerners in certain states and situations were excluded. Even after taking an ironclad test oath, swearing innocence concerning rebellion, the citizens could be forbidden to own property, vote, or hold office.[62] Many faced financial ruin and a lack of opportunity to rebuild their lives, as the devastated South became more lawless. Fleeing from the consequences seemed a better, if not just as challenging, option.

While the United States was occupied with the War Between the States, Napoleon III, elected president and self-declared emperor of France, seized the opportunity to occupy Mexico using the pretense of collecting a bad debt owed to several European countries. French troops landed at Vera Cruz in December of 1861 and marched toward the capitol of Mexico City, but a pocket of resistance stood in the way. On May 5, 1862 (later commemorated as the Cinco de Mayo celebration), French soldiers attacked the historic town of Puebla but when repelled by the Mexicans, the invaders retreated. Almost a year later, the French were more aggressive and laid siege to Puebla. After two months, the Mexican forces surrendered. Mexican defender Benito Juarez withdrew his government north to San Luis Potosi.

Over the next six months, the French claimed much of the country. About the same time, Ridgely Greathouse was re-arrested in Yreka as a dangerous criminal. On March 12, 1864, Archduke Ferdinand Maximilian of Austria accepted from Napoleon III the title of the Emperor of Mexico. Later that year, on November 13, the French Navy bombarded Mazatlán. Lesser-equipped Mexican forces once again withdrew. Mazatlán, which had been occupied by

---

62. Rolle, Andrew. *The Lost Cause: The Confederate Exodus to Mexico* (Norman: University of Oklahoma, 1992).

the United States during its war with Mexico in 1847, was declared officially a French colony. Hostilities continued, and many towns in the home state of Sinaloa were looted and burned. Mazatlán was known as the Pearl of the Pacific, the port of many nationalities (because of its popularity with adventurers), and also a gateway to lucrative silver mines to plunder.

On April 9, 1865, Robert E. Lee surrendered on behalf of the Confederacy to General U.S. Grant, marking the official end to the Civil War. Less than a week later, John Wilkes Boothe, a member of a particular "castle" or cell of the Knights of the Golden Circle, assassinated President Lincoln. According to *The Private Journal and Diary of John H. Surrant, A Conspirator*,[63] the KGC plotted a kidnapping of Lincoln even before he was inaugurated in 1861, but Boothe, obsessed with killing the President, shot him on April 15, 1865. Anyone who had actively participated in the rebellion, and even allegedly participated in the plot, was sure to face the threats of reprisal, prosecution, and capital punishment. Anticipating the worst, many Confederate cabinet members, military officers, soldiers, governors, and citizens left their war-torn country for perceived safer havens of Canada, England, Venezuela, Brazil, and Mexico.

As word of Lee's surrender filtered down to Confederate General "Jo" Shelby, he and some of his troops vowed to never surrender. With his Missouri Cavalry volunteers, Shelby marched through Texas, stopping to establish order as needed. At the border, they buried their tattered Confederate flag in the muddy waters of the Rio Grande as they crossed into Mexico. Shelby's troops were conflicted about which side of the Mexican war to support, and al-

---

63. Surratt, John H. *The Private Journal & Diary of John H. Surratt, the Conspirator* (New York: Fredrick A. Brady, 1866), pp. 28-29, 81-89. https://archive.org/details/privatejournaldi00surr

though Shelby favored throwing in with Benito Juarez's defenders, his men voted to support the royalty of the Emperor Maximilian and Queen Carlota.

Dr. William M. Gwin, former California Senator, offered his services to Maximilian to develop resources in return for establishing a colony in Sonora, but was rebuffed. William Maury had better luck and was awarded a tract of 500,000 acres for new immigrants to the so-called Carlota's Colony. Those lured away from Reconstruction retaliation in the South to land grants in Mexico faced cultural, medical, physical, and mental hardships in attempting to establish their isolated homesteads in a country foreign to them, both geographically and culturally. Severe challenges came from the displaced indigenous people, the jungle environment, the prolonged rainy season with attendant diseases such as yellow fever and malaria, as well as a shortage of labor and supplies. Eventually, the withdrawal of French support brought death-dealing attacks on the colonists from the Indians and bandits.

On May 29, 1865, Andrew Johnson's Amnesty Proclamation offered a general pardon to those who had continued to participate in the rebellion after Lincoln's proclamations but later had a change of heart and desired to apply for and obtain amnesty and a pardon. Among those excluded from the pardon were agents of the pretended Confederate states and those absent from the U.S. for the purpose of aiding the rebellion. Ridge Greathouse was still on the run.

Pearl of the Pacific

In the summer of 1865, Ridgely sailed to the west coast of Mexico, where he joined a group of Confederates-in-exile at Mazatlán.

The port of many nationalities had been controlled by pirates and various governments of the Spanish, the British, the United States, and the French. Not to mention, one of the first traders came from the Philippines bringing supplies for the silver mines. By 1836, a steady trade with Germany served a population of about 4,000-5,000 non-natives. Forty-Niners arrived at Vera Cruz and spent weeks traveling overland to Mazatlán, where they would embark for San Francisco. German immigrants of the 1850s left their imprint on the culture with beer, music, and place-names. Ice, another innovation influenced by foreigners, was brought in from San Francisco and stored in tunnels on Ice House Hill. When the French bombarded the port in 1864, three hotels and three restaurants served Mazatlán, the capital of the state of Sinaloa.

"Large numbers of disbanded soldiers of the late Confederacy are pouring into Northern Mexico. General David S. Terry, with a train including his own and several families, have arrived at Sonora by the way of Chihuahua. Colonel Dan Showalter, Colonel Kennedy, Ridgely Greathouse, Duncan Beaumont, and hundreds of others are at Mazatlán, and several thousands in all are scattered through these northern departments," reported the San Francisco newspapers on the week of August 30, 1865.[64]

David Terry had broken the law and was disgraced by participating in a death-wielding duel, as had Dan Showalter in a separate incident. As a Californian assemblyman in 1861, Showalter dueled with a fellow legislator and, as a result, killed him. Fleeing the law, Showalter slipped out of the state and joined up with about 18 men who planned to join the Confederacy in Texas. They were intercepted

---

64. "The Latest Gwin Story," *San Franciso Examiner*, August 30, 1865. https://www.news-papers.com/

and captured by Union soldiers with orders to stop anyone on the way to aid the Rebels. For five months, the group was detained in the Territorial Prison at Yuma, Arizona. Upon taking the oath of allegiance to the United States, they were released and traveled back to Drum Barracks near Los Angeles to pick up their gear.

Not to be deterred from their mission, the group left and went directly into Mexico and then east to Texas to join the 4th Texas Cavalry of the Arizona Brigade. Showalter quickly rose through the ranks to lieutenant colonel, counted victories at Galveston and Sabine Pass, and cleared the lower Rio Grande Valley of Union troops in 1864. When his commander, John Salmon Ford, fell ill, Showalter was so drunk he was unable to assume command. Several months later at the Battle of Palmito Hill, he was again so drunk he was unable to assume command under enemy fire.

When Showalter was relieved of his command and sent to San Antonio for court-martial, his command was given to Major F.E. Kavanaugh. Despite the charges, Showalter escaped punishment and returned to his command. Although Robert E. Lee surrendered in April 1865, the Texas Rebels did not stand down until June. At that point, many supporters of the Confederacy, officials, governors, and military officers, including Showalter, headed for Mexico or other countries for fear of imprisonment or worse for their part in the rebellion. Some had their homes and estates destroyed during the war, while other sympathizers faced confiscation of property and assets by the government. When desperate men, hardened by war, congregated anywhere, even in Mazatlán, the Pearl of the Pacific, trouble followed.

A correspondent from Mazatlán to San Francisco's *Daily Alta California* noted on November 19, 1865, "The new firm of Showalter,

Greathouse & Company commenced business in the hotel line yesterday. I am unable to send you a description of the building, furniture, etc., by this steamer, but will do so in the next. Suffice it to say that it is to be called the Ox Hide and Tail House: location, Villa de Union, Presidio."[65] The hotel was located in a village 12 miles southeast of the area of Centro in Mazatlán. The name "Greathouse & Company" lends credence that the visit of George Greathouse from California supplied the investment money from the brothers' partnership. That money was held in common for the good of all, according to Ridge's own account in his 1868 interview with O'Meara.[66]

Showalter involved another partner in the hotel/saloon, the Ox Hide and the Tail. That partner was F.E. Kavanaugh, the major who took over Showalter's command in the 4th Texas Cavalry. When an argument ensued between the two, Kavanaugh and Showalter got into a fight, and Showalter was wounded. An infection set in, and on March 4, 1866, Dan Showalter died of lockjaw. Kavanaugh died of undisclosed reasons later in the same year, and he was buried in Mexico City.[67]

With the end of the Civil War, the United States sent troops to the northern border of Mexico and funneled weapons to Benito Juarez's Mexican Juarista forces in an effort to discourage Maximilian's imperialist troops. From pressure exerted by the U.S., Napoleon III

---

65. *Daily Alta California*, San Francisco Nov. 19, 1865. Accessed October 7, 2020. https://cdnc.ucr.edu/?a=d&d=DAC18651119&e=-------en--20-1--txt-txIN--------1

66. O'Meara, James. "A Notable Escape," *The Californian*, Vol. 28, April 1882, pp. 342, 347, accessed April 16, 2020. California State Library/LSTA Grant.

67. Bailey, Christopher H. *The Stulls of "Millsborough," A Genealogical History of John Stull, "the Miller," Pioneer of Western Maryland*, Vol. 1 (C.H. Bailey; limited first edition, January 2000). Microfilm item #6, Project and Roll #530, G.S. Call # 1425443, y lib us can. Also can be viewed online at https://www.familysearch.org/library/books/records/item/420731-redirection

ordered withdrawal of French forces on May 31, 1866. When the French Navy took the port of Mazatlán in 1862, a new war zone was created for citizens and Confederate exiles in the state of Sinaloa. Exactly four years to the day from that date, on November 13, 1866, Mexican General Ramon Corona expelled the French. Once again in control of the Mexicans were the roads through Durango and over the Sierra Madre Occidental to Monterey. *Without a pardon in his pocket, would this be the time and the challenging route for Ridge Greathouse to slip undetected into the southern border of Texas? There is no record for how he arrived in Texas.*

Maximilian's troubled and bloody reign of only four years ended when the French-declared emperor was executed on June 19, 1867, in Queretaro, Mexico. This was a strong statement that Mexico would not tolerate government interference by foreign powers. In that same year of 1867, President Andrew Johnson invoked the Monroe Doctrine to further discourage foreign intervention anywhere in North America. By that time, Ridge had a new plan to get back into the states, and it involved his brother Robert in Gonzales, Texas.

Points of Interest

1. El Paso to Mazatlan Road
2. Mazatlan to Monterrey Road
3. Mexico City, Capitol
4. Carlotta's Colonies
5. Port of Veracruz
6. Port of Galveston

13. Routes to Mazatlán and to South Texas.

CHAPTER 9

Cattle Frontier

The iconic longhorn, a naturalized feral breed of Spanish cattle, thrived in the semi-tropical coastal grasslands of South Texas, where the Guadalupe River meandered through Gonzales County. With an annual growing season of 270 days, the thick grasses supported large herds of cattle and mustang. Oaks and pecans lined the streambeds along the rich bottomlands, providing food for wildlife and attracting Native Americans, as well as white settlers.

The feisty town of Gonzales became known in 1835 as the "first Lexington" of the Texas Revolution when Mexican dragoons showed up to retrieve a cannon loaned for the settlers' protection against the Indians. The citizens of Gonzales defiantly yelled, "Come and take it!" at the Mexican soldiers who retreated. This stiff-backed resistance caught on as the Republic of Texas declared its independence from Mexico in 1836. With Sam Houston as commander, the rebels suffered many setbacks: the loss of the fortress Alamo, the Runaway Scrape of fleeing civilians, and a turn-tail retreat with his volunteer soldiers. Finally, Houston turned to face the enemy and led the volunteer army of Texans to a surprising 18-minute battle victory at San Jacinto, culminating in the capture of Santa Anna, the president of Mexico. While Indians continued to harass, capture, or kill settlers on the Texas frontier, the whites' Council House attack on several Comanche chiefs in San Antonio brought a savage retaliation. Comanches swept down the Guadalupe Valley in 1840, killing settlers, stealing horses, and plundering and burning settlements. Enraged citizens rushed to punish the warriors in the Battle of Plum Creek, forcing the Indians to the western frontier.

Into this less-than-idyllic frontier environment came Henry Greathouse in 1858, to invest in a ranch on behalf of his brothers. He brought the youngest brother, Robert Langhorne, 21, with him.

The following year, Henry registered as an agent for R.L. and Bill Greathouse and paid taxes in Gonzales County on a ranch consisting of 176 acres with 100 head of cattle.[68] The ranch was surrounded by plenty of free open-range grazing. Although almost a third of the population in Gonzales County and one-half in Lavaca County were slaves, in 1860 Robert Greathouse reported only one 15-year-old slave, who registered four years later as a black man under the name of Bill Greathouse.

Before Henry headed back to California with his family of five, he was listed on the 1860 tax assessment in Gonzales County with real property of 177 acres, valued at $1,000 or $5.65 per acre. Robert's personal property that year listed one Negro valued at $1,200, 32 horses at $820, and 800 head of cattle at $4,800[69] or $6 a head. With land from original grantor Eli Mitchell and a promising ranch setup, Robert married Marcella Jones, daughter of

---

68. Tax rolls of 1860, Gonzales County, Texas.

69. Assessment of property situated in Gonzales County, Texas, Real and Personal Property, 1860.

surveyor William B. Jones of Gonzales, on September 19, 1860. In the next several years, R. L. Greathouse claimed 315 acres of land and herds ranging up to 2,000 head. With such a small investment in land and by carrying that many cattle, Robert was utilizing the open range and increasing his herd by rounding up the wild and wily longhorns.

War Comes to Texas

With the Texas secession from the Union, young men who were moved by patriotism and the lure of adventure joined up all over the state. Recruited by Captain Hess Jones, Robert enrolled in Company E of the 21st Texas Cavalry, known as Carter's Lancers. In the tradition of Sir Lancelot, the mounted unit practiced jousting, but the lances never materialized. However, each candidate was ordered to "furnish his own horse, the best he can procure, two suits of winter clothing, a bowie knife, and the best firearms he can obtain: if possible, a double-barrel shotgun, and six shooter."[70]

At the time of Robert's enrollment on March 14, 1862, the response was so great that three regiments were formed. The 26-year-old rode 125 miles to the rendezvous point near Hempstead, where he was mustered in at Camp Carter. Assigned to the Arkansas battle line, the Texas Lancers regiment fought under duress, with some captured and sent to Union POW camps before an exchange. The surviving remnant was assigned to Parson's Cavalry Brigade in October of 1862.

Records for Robert are very limited, but the final muster roll dated August 31, 1862, to February 25, 1863, stated that he was

---

70. "To the Chivalry of Texas, a printed call to form a cavalry." Bullock Museum, Austin. https://www.thestoryoftexas.com/

on sick furlough since October 15, 1862. Hopefully, he made it home for the birth of his second child two weeks later. In late 1863, each unit was ordered to its home county to arrest deserters and draft evaders. No record surfaced of Robert's return or arrest, but family accounts claim he provided several hundred head of cattle to the Confederate Army for which he received partial payment in Confederate greenbacks and fruitless promises for payment of the remainder after the war.[71]

The South was running out of men, supplies, and arms as the 21st Texas Cavalry participated in the invasion of Missouri, helped chase the Union Army into retreat down the Red River in 1864, and participated in the last battle at Yellow Bayou in 1864. The unit was disbanded in the spring of 1864.[72] Although Lee surrendered the Army of Virginia in April of 1865, some Texan troops did not stand down until June.

To Go or Stay

From California, George Greathouse wrote to their recently widowed older sister, Sarah Belle Greathouse Young, asking if the conditions in Kentucky would allow a return to their home country. Belle responded to George, lamenting the shape of the farms and the impossibility of finding even immigrant labor to raise crops.

She wrote on January 29, 1866, "Why haven't you thought of going to Mexico & joining Price & Shelby's colony? People here are talking of going. They furnish land gratis, & I would think the

71. Howes, Edward H. and Benjamin F. Gilbert, editors, "Land and Labor in Kentucky, 1865; Letters to George Lewis Greathouse." *The Register of the Kentucky Historical Society*, Vol. 48, No. 162 (January 1950), pp. 25-31.
72. Bailey, Anne J., "Twenty-First Texas Cavalry," *Handbook of Texas Online*, accessed October 7, 2020. https://www.tshaonline.org/handbook/entries/twenty-first-texas-cavalry

society would be so fine. If Robt. is determined to move, & Ridge cannot come into the U.S., why don't you all agree to go to Mexico, & I would go too. What does Ridge write on the subject? Don't let him come into the States, even with a pardon. Semmes was paroled, but they disregarded that, & now they have him in prison. Ridge must have some personal enemy that persecuted him so. Joshua Tevis said he thought he [Ridge] had one in Lincoln's cabinet—let me know how to get letters to him without troubling Coz Lloyd . . . P.S. Write—what do you think of going to Mexico? Is the government too unstable?"[73]

Neither George nor other family members followed their brother into exile in Mexico, a country that was fighting its own civil war with Confederates split between the Mexican Juaristas and the French imperialists. Former CSA Generals Sterling Price and Jo Shelby, along with 30 other prominent exiles, were indeed attracting Southerners to Carlota's Colony, only three days' ride from Mexico City. Not until September 1867 would President Johnson issue a second proclamation, a general amnesty for some war criminals, but not Ridgely Greathouse.

The conflict between the French and Mexicans crept into the countryside outside Mazatlán. Following the withdrawal of the French troops in 1866, the political climate of the port changed. The benefits of living within the enclave of Villa Union, 12 miles from historic Mazatlán, were altered. In the exodus of exiles from the port, perhaps Ridge and others followed the overland road, previously used by Confederates, to backtrack to Durango, then go through Torreon, Saltillo, and Monterey, over the permeable

73. "Land and Labor in Kentucky, 1865; Letters to George Lewis Greathouse," Howes, Edward H. and Benjamin F. Gilbert, editors. *The Register of the Kentucky Historical Society*, Vol. 48, No. 162 (January 1950), pp. 25-31.

border near Nuevo Laredo. From there a well-worn bandido trail led through the Wild Horse Desert to Lavaca County and neighboring Gonzales County. *Or, as reported in Hotel Arrivals in the local Galveston newspaper, did the fact that R.L. Greathouse had checked into the Crawford House in Galveston on December 14 and 20, 1866,*[74] *indicate that Ridge planned to enter at the Texas coastal port and join his brother there?*

74. "Hotel Arrivals," Flake's Bulletin, Galveston, Texas. Vol II, Issue 151, pg. 5; Vol. II, Issue 156, p. 1. GenealogyBank.

CHAPTER 10

Long Trail Ahead

Whatever the circumstances or the location, Ridge secretly slipped back into Texas and joined his brother Robert at the Greathouse ranch. (*A Bill Greathouse was listed on a poll tax list in 1866. Was this the black, now freed man, Bill Greathouse voting, or was this an alias for Ridge, a man with a quirky sense of humor who was denied the right to vote due to his criminal record?*)

A man who championed big schemes, Ridge and his younger brother were making plans to cash in by supplying beef to north-western markets. Their eyes were on Idaho, where their brothers were hauling freight, mail, and people along stagecoach routes in the mining country. Fresh beef would bring high prices in mining country, considerably more than the $6 a head at the oversupplied trail head. It was the plan of a capitalist.

While Texans were engaged in war with many away from their homes, the Texas longhorn prospered and proliferated on the coastal grasslands and the semitropical climate. The animals had long been a readily available resource for Mexicans in the hide and tallow trade. Tough and disease resistant by natural selection, the cattle were lean but fattened well on northern ranges. During the Republic of Texas (1836 to 1845), cattle were driven to markets in New Orleans and as far as Oregon or Ohio. In the 1850s, cattle were driven along the Texas Trail (aka the Kansas Trail) to points north of Indian Territory. As the country settled up, trails altered to allow grazing or to avoid the settlers' domestic cattle, which were not immune to tick fever and often died from exposure to the ticks. After the Civil War, former soldiers or unemployed young men, white and black, were looking for jobs or to turn a profit and sought cow hunts and cattle drives. The untended and unbranded livestock, considered wild game, was free for the taking. The challenge was getting the wily longhorns to their destination.

14. Cattle drive. Art by Kayla White.

Because of downright hostile opposition in allowing contagious tick-infested longhorns to cross their country in eastern Kansas,

Joseph McCoy advertised in 1867 that his isolated cattle depot on the Kansas Pacific Railroad welcomed the Texas longhorns. He sent flyers and posted notices in newspapers far and wide. Likely the notices caught the attention of Robert Greathouse, but his destination was Idaho.

Forming a crew on May 6, 1867, Robert began the difficult task of rounding up 2,000 head of cattle scattered over the open range shared with his neighbors, the Mitchells and the Mooneys. Once on the trail, a crew of about 10 could handle that many cattle with a trail boss, a foreman, a cook, six or so drovers, and a horse wrangler to tend to 20 or 30 horses. Columbus "Lump" Mooney and Chauncey Abrams Mitchell, whose father, Eli, originally owned the Greathouse property, were part of the crew ready to leave Gonzales County on June 5, 1867.[75] In a letter written along the trail to his wife, Marcella, at home, Robert mentioned that his brother Ridge was on the cattle drive and doing well.[76]

By following an early trace out of Gonzales County, Robert piloted his cattle north. Barring any unforeseen circumstances, grazing and walking about 10 miles a day, the herd could arrive in Kansas by June or July and Idaho by winter. Likely the herd crossed the Colorado River at Austin, picked up the trail at Waco, and then took the west branch near Fort Worth, crossed into Oklahoma

75. Boethel, Paul. *On the Headwaters of the Lavaca and the Navidad* (Austin: Von Boeckmann-Jones, 1967). This date was also verified in a letter that Marcella wrote in 1889 to a long-time friend, Mrs. M.B. (Mary) West that is provided by French Simpson Memorial Library, Halletsville, Texas, 77964.

76. Greathouse-L archives, "William Greathouse and Descendants," Letter from David McLeod Greathouse to John D. Greathouse, September 27, 1999. http://archiver.rootsweb.ancestry.com/th/read/GREATHOUSE/1999-09/0938490830
Also, Rebecca Greathouse Wren to Marisue Potts, concerning Robert's letter to Marcella, which had been in possession of her father, David McLeod Greathouse, email May 10, 2012.

Territory at Red River Station, and headed toward Fort Arbuckle in Indian Territory. The fort, built to protect reservation Indians from hostile Plains tribes, was protected by black recruits known as Buffalo Soldiers. Leaving the fort, the trail toward Idaho veered toward Dodge City for resupply before hitting the California Trail and westward bound. It was a long, dangerous trip.

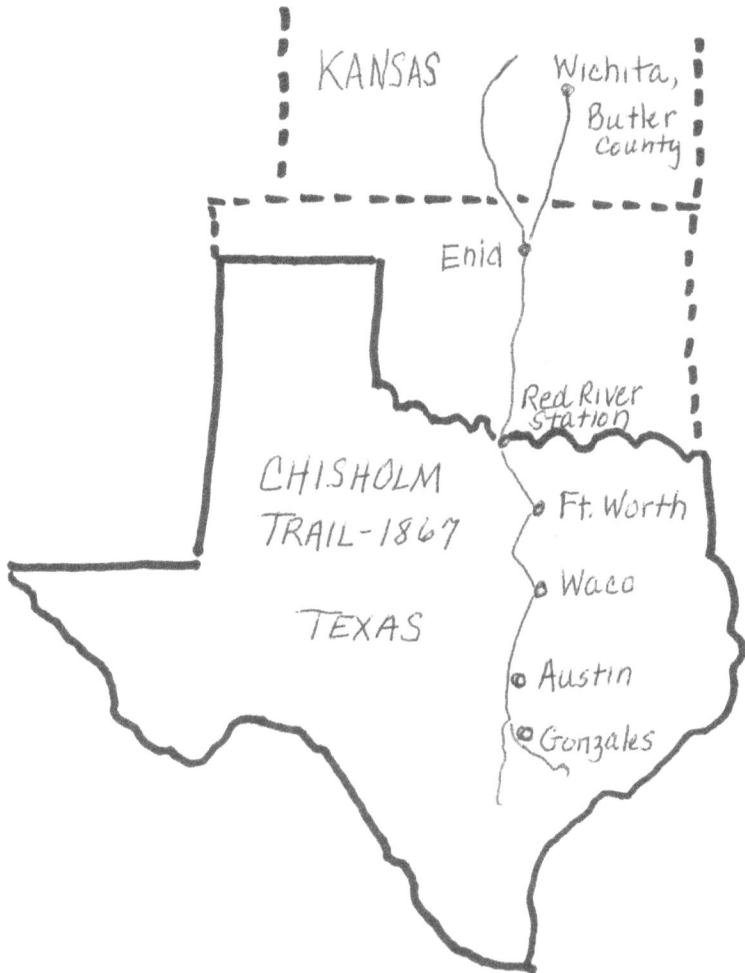

15. Chisholm Trail from Gonzales, Texas, to Wichita, Kansas.

What Robert's crew faced likely coincided with that of Colonel O.W. Wheeler who also left with a herd in 1867.[77] The Chisholm Trail was but a whisper at the time, a trace that led to a freighter's trail, but the dangers, known or unknown, were real. According to Wheeler, his drovers faced the threat of unfriendly Indians, thunderstorms, swollen rivers, "washy" grass lacking in nutrition, and frightening stampedes. Their most severe threat, however, hit with a deadly cholera epidemic that was sweeping the country. On July 3, 1867, cholera struck the soldiers at Fort Arbuckle, then Fort Gibson, and then Fort Smith. The disease prevailed among the tribes of the Cherokee, Creek, Caddo, Comanche, Seminole, Delaware, Shawnee, and Wichita. The headwaters of the Big Bear Creek became known as Skeleton Creek for the bones of the Wichita tribe members found along its banks. In Ellsworth, Kansas, a fast-moving, deadly strain absolutely threw the settlement of 1,000, into a panic, with desertion of all but 40, who were the very brave or foolish.[78]

For the Greathouse crew, cholera dealt the deadman's hand. The "blue death," so named for the bluish hue of the skin due to dehydration caused by vomiting and diarrhea, was a sanitation disease, caused from eating food or drinking water contaminated by feces of an infected person. Without treatment, the disease progressed quickly, leaving the victim with a sunken, hollowed-eyed look before dying. A newspaper account from his hometown of Maysville, Kentucky, recounts Robert's difficulties. "While on a drive with thousands of cattle to Idaho, cholera broke out among

77. Gray, Jim, "The Makings of a Trail Blazer, Col. O.W. Wheeler," *Kansas Cowboy*, July-August 2008. kansascowboy@kans.com

78. Gray, Jim. *Desperate Seed: Ellsworth Kansas on the Violent Frontier* (Ellsworth: Kansas Cowboy Publications, 2009), p. 10-11; Gray, Jim, "The Way West," *Chase County Leader-News*, January 5, 2017.

his drovers, and they became panic-stricken and most of them deserted him. He was left almost alone, and had to swim a river twice, carrying a man on his back either time. The exposure brought on an attack of the cholera, from which he died, without any attention, and was buried wrapped only in his blanket and in the same grave as one of his men."[79]

Likely, that other casualty buried with Robert was Americus Mooney, whose brother Columbus was on the cattle drive with the Greathouses. The Mooney family lists the death date of Americus as August 14, 1867, in Butler County, Kansas. The railhead cattle shipping point of Wichita was located in Butler County, but the grave location of both Americus and Robert remained unknown. Columbus Mooney and Chauncey Mitchell were able to return home to Gonzales County, where they lived out their lives.

Ridge may have been the other stricken man that Robert attempted to save by swimming the river. Survivors of cholera exhibit a gray, ashen pallor with very wrinkled skin, muscular difficulties, and difficulty in talking, among other symptoms.[80] By nature a fearless man of implicit confidence, Ridge was noted in O'Meara's 1868 interview in Idaho City, Idaho, as being bruised in spirit and without heart for the joys of life. "His clear, blue eyes worn to leaden hue and haggard expression; his face wrinkled and grooved into deep, hard lines, his cheery tone of voice fallen to a low, gruff monotone; his light smart step altered to a sluggish, draggling pace; and his glad, inspiring presence and manner past all recall, in the gloomy

79. "Robert Greathouse," *The Evening Bulletin*, Maysville, Kentucky) 1887-1905, July 19, 1902, Image 3. http://chroniclingamerica.loc.gov/lccn/sn87060190/1902-07-19/ed-1/seq-3/

80. "Cholera Throughout History," *Encyclopaedia Britannica*, accessed November 11, 2020. https://www.britannica.com/science/cholera/Cholera-through-history

indifference and the soured and saddened nature which seemed incapable of mirth."[81]

Swimming the river twice under duress likely hastened Robert's demise. If the crew was as fearful of catching the disease as those who abandoned Ellsworth, Kansas, they scattered to the four winds, leaving Ridgely or someone else to dispose of the herd or abandon it and ride away. On August 24, 1867, Marcella, the mother of three small children with one on the way, received a telegram with the news of Robert's death in Kansas.[82] If the two 19-year-olds, Columbus Mooney and Chauncey Mitchell, became ill, they recovered and eventually returned to Gonzales, leaving in Kansas the unmarked grave of their herd boss and the brother of Columbus.

In the spring, Marcella petitioned the court[83] to sell 150 head of cattle to pay expenses to bring Robert's body back, but neither tombstone nor record of either burial was found. Despite the hardships of losing her husband and the cattle in the trail drive, Mrs. R.L. Greathouse declared 2,500 head of cattle on the 1869 tax rolls of Lavaca County,[84] where 56,000 head were estimated the following year. The much larger neighboring Gonzales County, with its 19,807 square miles, estimated 75,000 head in 1870 before 40,000 were gathered and sent to northern markets.[85]

---

81. O'Meara, James. "A Notable Escape," *The Californian*, Vol. 28, April 1882, p. 343, accessed April 16, 2020. California State Library/LSTA Grant.

82. Boethel, Paul. *On the Headwaters of the Lavaca and the Navidad* (Austin: Von Boeckmann-Jones, 1967).

83. Lavaca County probate records, Probate #303, R.L. Greathouse, March 31, 1868.

84. Lavaca County tax assessment, Real and Personal Property, 1869.

85. Long, Christopher, "Lavaca County," *Handbook of Texas Online*, accessed April 15, 2010, https://www.tshaonline.org/handbook/entries/lavaca-county; Baumgartner, Dorcas Huff and Genevieve B. Vollentine, "Gonzales County," accessed April 15, 2020. https://www.tshaonline.org/handbook/entries/gonzales-county

Before heading for Idaho to reunite with his other brothers, Ridge, the grieving and possibly recuperating survivor, journeyed to his old home in Kentucky to be consoled by family and friends. Many questions were left unanswered. All that is certain is Ridgely Greathouse had made another miraculous escape.

16. Ridge Greathouse.

CHAPTER 11

Winding Roads to and From Idaho

If a trail drive of 2,000-3,000 head of cattle left from Gonzales in May (or June) with the cattle walking 10 miles a day, grazing and resting as they traveled north, they might arrive in Kansas in two to three months. The length of time depended on the weather, stampedes, delays in getting permission to cross through Indian Territory, or other unforeseen circumstances, like illness.

A possible scenario is this: After Ridge buried his brother Robert and left or disposed of the cattle, he sent Marcella a telegram on August 27, 1867. If Ridge came in "under the wire" to Texas before being pardoned, it seems doubtful he'd go back south to Texas, but head north as planned. He might need a week to take the Kansas Pacific Railroad to the east, then go to Louisville and overland to Mason County, Kentucky. A visit with family might take two or three weeks. Anticipating the closing of mountain roads due to snow drifts, he would try to arrive in Idaho before late 1867.

What is known is this: After visiting Kentucky friends and family, Ridge continued to Idaho to join George, the banker who had relocated from California, and Henry, who had sold his stage line business running from Boise into the Boise Basin. Ridgely, age 38, had become well established in Idaho City, Boise County, according to the 1870 census. He listed his profession as a banker and declared his personal property to be valued at $17,000. George, also a banker, and his wife listed six children, ages 3 to 13. Henry, the stage line proprietor, was 40, and he and his second wife Jane McCall listed three children, a stage driver, a farm worker, a bookkeeper, and a laborer in their household.

As busy as they were with making money in a myriad of ways, the Greathouse men did take time off. The winters were usually mild in the Boise Basin until past the middle of January when it was not unusual for the mercury to drop well below zero, with snow blocking the roads until March. The down time for man and beast provided a time to get away. Many miners went east or into Colorado, Utah, or Oregon. Henry and his wife took off from Boise City in October for a health-seeking pleasure trip to the Sandwich Islands. On February 3, 1871, the newsy *Owyhee Avalanche Journal* reported that Ridgley Greathouse of the banking firm Greathouse and Brothers had gone to Mexico for health, and his brother George for the same reason.

An anecdote from the *Idaho Statesman* newspaper peels back the veneer on the character of Ridgely Greathouse. "In the early days when John Lemp first started his brewery in this city, his capital was rather limited and he felt that the high price of barley and hops would compel him to count his quarters closely. The big glasses at 25 cents, or two bits a drink, measured out the beer profusely, but John concluded he would have to stand it if the rest did. He had not been long in the business before a splendid customer in the person of Rigby [sic] Greathouse, who had started a bank a few doors above him. Rigby [sic] came often and drank beer every time, but always put down two short bits—two 10 cent pieces. John said he would not have cared so much, but he was satisfied that Greathouse knew just what he was making and intended to break him up in business. It was a nip and tuck game between them. The bank, however, closed up its business after a year or two and he [Lemp] never again had so exacting a customer."[86]

Looking for new frontiers other than coaching, Henry, with his family and their two wagons, joined up with eight other wagons to head for Texas in the spring of 1872. Since there was no banking exchange between different sections of the country, several families carried a considerable amount of cash with them over some 1,300 trail miles. The Greathouse family had hidden $50,000 under the floorboards of one of their wagons. Upon arrival in Texas, Henry scouted around and decided that Decatur, Wise County, on the old Chisholm Trail was just the place to start a bank.

Henry's investigation led him to believe the government would soon have the Indians well in hand. The army officers at nearby Fort Richardson assured him that the frontier would be protected at all costs, and that if he desired to make any investments, it was the right time to do so. Arabella Fulton, who wrote of the move from Idaho, described Henry Greathouse as a very conservative man, not given to injudicious advice, and very dependable.[87] His banking interests, financed with the money hidden underneath the planks of the family's wagon, did well, and his bank became the forerunner of the First National Bank of Decatur.

---

86. *Idaho Semi-Weekly World*, Idaho City, Idaho, August 31, 1875.
87. Fulton, Arabella Clemens. *Tales of the Trail* (Caldwell: B. C. Payette, 1965; Wise County Heritage Museum, Decatur, Texas).

Still searching for his own opportunities in Idaho, Ridgely was 250 miles from home in Winnemucca, Nevada. He was seeking stock to buy for the meat-hungry miners in Idaho. In the Red Bluff area in California, where he once carried gold dust and passengers by mule trains over the mountain trails, he found it overstocked with sheep. A large flock could be handled by just a few people trailing them into Idaho Territory. The owner of such livestock was bound to make money. Just a month later, the *Idaho Statesman* noted he'd returned with 3,050 head of sheep.[88]

Three years later, Ridgely was granted a patent for 73 acres in Ada County, Idaho Territory, through the U.S. Land Office. Many miners bought land to hold their claims, but Idaho City lots were so rich in ore yields that people dug underneath their homes. On May 31, 1875, the *Owyhee Avalanche News* noted Ridgley Greathouse, George Washington Stilts, and several other old-timers left on a prospecting expedition among the Wagon Town bonanzas. "They intend to be absent ten days and during that time expect to stride the mammoth ledge of the new district." The Wagon Town bonanzas attracted thousands—but most of the claims were already secured, and the latecomers either left or scattered all over the countryside.

For the rest of the year, August to December 1875, Ridgely was making $125 a month as an express manager for Wells Fargo at Silver City, going by stage to Winnemucca and back. In August a column in an Idaho City newspaper opined, "George L. Greathouse Esq. and his estimable family will take their departure from Silver City by stage to take up residence at Santa Rosa, California. They will be greatly missed in the social circles of Silver City, and our town

---

88. *Idaho Statesman*, November 4, 1871.

will lose a good citizen and an upright honorable businessman."[89] In December, R. Greathouse was no longer employed by the Wells Fargo & Company as a messenger.

Like a shiny penny, the personable Ridgley kept turning up in the local newspaper gossip columns. In September 1876 he was spotted in Boise City. Several months later in December, Ridgley Greathouse was elected doorkeeper of the Idaho Legislative House, with 15 votes, compared to four for his opponent. The *Owyhee Avalanche* reported that the organization of the House officials, some who came from long distances with great expectations, included bread-and-butter patriots hoping to secure minor offices. The gossipy paper related, "Ridge was quite elated over his success and immediately proceeded to draw a requisition on the Governor for postage stamps for the members, but the functionary informed him that the stamps would come in good time through the regular source."[90] More seriously, as doorkeeper, Ridge's duties were to control access to the senate sessions, maintain order in the galleries, provide security for the senators, and detain or arrest anyone who violated senate rules.

Although he seemed to be enjoying his life in Idaho, the death of his older brother and long-time protector, George Lewis Greathouse, in 1879 in Santa Rosa, California, surely affected Ridge. Speculation within family accounts next placed Ridgely with Henry in Wise County, Texas. If his personality remained the same as he aged, a good guess is he did not stay long in Decatur, where his wealthy relatives threw lawn parties and entertained lavishly. If his personality

89. *Idaho Semi-weekly World,* Idaho City, Idaho, August 31, 1875. https://www.news-papers.com/

90. "Legislative," *Owyhee Daily Avalanche News*, December 9, 1876. http://www.gene-alogybank.com/gbnk/newspapers/doc

stayed the same, Ridgely headed for another frontier, perhaps the rolling plains and the Caprock region. There, forced removal of the Comanches in 1875 had been accelerated by an influx of buffalo hunters who were killing off the Native Americans' commissary.

The hunters and skinners gambled with their lives that they could make a year's wages with just a few months of hard work, *if* they survived renegade Indians, thieves, accidents, and illness. Coincidentally, Napoleon Bonaparte "Arkansas Jack" Greathouse, a distant cousin from the Arkansas family branch, was hunting in the vicinity of John Cook's camp in 1876, near a location that Ridgely would later travel as an exterminator of lobo wolves, coyotes, and prairie dogs. In the area, also, Whiskey Jim Greathouse was a character around the buffalo hunters' outpost of Rath City. His unhealthy habit of stealing horses and then asking for a reward upon their return kept Whiskey Jim in trouble. He participated with other buffalo hunters in the melee pursuit of Indians in the Yellowhouse Canyon skirmish and became involved with Billy the Kid and other outlaws in New Mexico.

Although some Greathouse kin left tracks, the whereabouts of Ridgely Greathouse for the next 20 years remains a mystery. With his propensity to travel, he could have been anywhere. The absence of the 1880 census provides no clues, no traces, no insights on how he was making a living, yet buffalo hunting, skinning, or freighting of the 1870s offered a quick way to make a lot of money fast, something a "capitalist" might do.

CHAPTER 12

Free-Ranging Buffalo to Free Range

After 20 years of silence and leaving no scent trail, Ridge Greathouse once again surfaced on the frontier of the buffalo range, which had turned into a free range bonanza for cattlemen. After many years of avoidance or isolation, Ridge was finally spotted in the census of 1900. The census taker caught up with him in Guthrie, King County, Texas, where he was boarding with the family of J.A. and Laura Franklin in their home. The hotel/boarding house let rooms and, if need be, turned the kids out of their rooms to sleep on pallets under the dining table while guests took their beds. The Franklins also had a camp house with a stove and a wagonyard for tending to saddle mounts or teams.[91] The other boarder listed his profession as "Cattle Raiser," and maybe that prompted 69-year-old Ridgely, a man without any property to declare, to proudly give his occupation as "Capitalist."[92]

Greathouse was in the middle of Burk Burnett's ranch country, and not far to the west was the Pitchfork Ranch and the Espuela

---

91. King County Historical Society, "John A. and Laura Franklin." *King County (Texas) Windmills and Barbed Wire* (Quanah: Nortex Press, 1976), pp. 254-256.

92. 1900 U.S. Federal Census for R. Greathouse, King County Texas, Comm. Pct. 01, Dist. 0021.

or Spur Ranch, and to the north was the Matador Ranch, which
sprawled over four counties. Greathouse was a welcome diversion,
if not an eccentric guest, at the ranch chuckwagons. He was a head-
scratching mystery, as well as high drama, within a small, isolated
community of cowboys who lived outdoors at the wagon and received only two days off every year: Christmas and Independence
Day. A "Ridge-sighting" was bound to be repeated and retold many
times for years. It soon became legend on the ranching frontier.

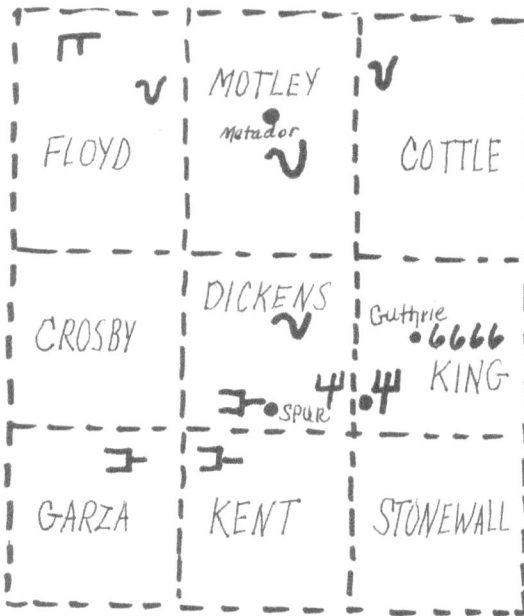

Early Ranch Ranges

- Lazy F Ranch
- Matador Cattle Company
- Pitchfork Ranch
- Espuela (Spur) Ranch
- Four Sixes Ranch

17. Free-range ranches of the Texas Rolling Plains.

With the former invasion of buffalo hunters desperate to participate in a short-lived boom economy, a gold rush of sorts had made short order of the massive southern herd that once supported the Plains tribes. An old folk song, "The Buffalo Skinners Lament," asked, "How do you do, young fellow, how would you like to go and spend the summer pleasantly on the range of the buffalo?" In the song, Buffalo Jack responded, "If you will pay good wages, transportation too, I will go with you on the range of the buffalo." Later, the skinner realizes: "Our meat it was buffalo hump and iron wedge bread, and all we had to sleep on was a buffalo robe for a bed. The fleas and graybacks worked on us; O boys, it was not slow. I tell you there's no worse hell on earth than the range of the damned old buffalo."[93]

Tacit and stated approval from the military and improved fire power quickly decimated the great herds to near extinction. The players in the buffalo hunting industry were mostly out of work. The mother lode had played out. With the range cleared of the buffalo herds, cattlemen were not far behind, looking for fresh ranges and free grass for the prolific accumulations of longhorns in South Texas.

Lobo wolves, which had followed the buffalo herds, found cattle an easy target. To protect their herds, ranchers hired men to trap or poison wolves and coyotes. Wolfers, as the men like Greathouse were called, skinned the wolves and any other varmints they killed and sold the pelts for money or traded for supplies. By this humble means, Ridge Greathouse eked out a living on the last frontier of Texas. Joining him were other frontier dissidents or out-of-work hunters or skinners like Bob Payne, who was camped with another

---

93. Lomax, John A., "Buffalo Skinners," *Cowboy Songs and Other Frontier Ballads* (New York: MacMillan Co., 1918).

hunter, Frank Collinson, on the Running Water Draw, the headwaters of the Fresh Water Fork of the Brazos.

Collinson reported that without the buffalo to skin and process, Payne was harvesting lobo wolves and coyotes for their pelts. A good gray wolf pelt brought $1.50 to $2.00 and a coyote, only half a dollar. Payne's technique was simple. He would shoot a mustang, poison the carcass, and leave it on the prairie. The hungry wolves consumed the poisoned horse flesh and died. He skinned the hides and staked them out, just as he had done with the buffalo hides. Collinson concluded, "Payne's wagon was stacked high with gray wolf and coyote pelts which he planned to haul to market. There must have been several thousand of them."[94]

The manager of the Spur Ranch in Dickens County hired a fellow to hunt the wolves with a pack of hounds for six months. The boss admitted that while the old wolfer did not catch that many, he sure made the wolves change locations, and therefore did the ranch a good service. From time to time, professional hunters and trappers located to the Spur Ranch pastures, supporting themselves by the scalp bounties and the sale of the hides they processed or the $5 a lobo pelt premium the ranch paid.[95] During prolonged droughts, cattle bogged down in the mud of dried-up water holes and became exhausted to the point of death. In a salvage effort, men were paid $1 for each cow hide skinned. Often their pay came in supplies from the ranch commissary.

While wolfers were successful and drastically cut down on the number of canines, then the rodent-like prairie dogs became a

---

94. Collinson, Frank. *Life in the Saddle* (Norman, Oklahoma: University of Oklahoma, 1963), p. 174.

95. Holden, William Curry. *The Spur Ranch: A Study of the Inclosed Ranch Phase of the Cattle Industry in Texas* (Boston: The Christopher Publishing House, 1934), p. 176.

menace and the species of prey. The Spur Ranch first became alarmed about the prairie dog infestation in 1888.[96] The small rodents lived in colonies and destroyed many acres of grass around their prairie dog towns. The mounds proved dangerous to both horses and cattle because stepping in a den hole or sunken tunnel could break a leg. Some cowboys died when their horses stumbled after falling into prairie dog holes.

The Spur (Espuela) Ranch hired men like Greathouse to poison the prairie dogs over thousands of acres of rangeland. One unidentified dog-poisoner killed out the dogs in the Spur pastures of Duck Creek, West Horse, Little Horse, Little Dockum, and Tap. The pastures contained about 60 sections, with a fourth to a third almost entirely ruined for grazing by the prairie dogs. In total, the Spur Ranch had poisoned about 300,000 acres prior to 1904, with some dog poisoners earning five cents for an acre of extermination.[97]

On January 20, 1901, Matador Land and Cattle Company ranch manager Arthur Ligertwood noted in his diary: "Greathouse brought in 63 coyote scalps and owes $4 in hides."[98] The manager also noted that Virgil Leonard brought in lobo pups and W.E. Parks, aka the Pitchfork Kid or Billy Partlow, who once made rounds with Greathouse, brought in lobo pup scalps from Croton Pasture. Other information in the following year's diary touched on community building for Matador when Ligertwood reported on March 24, 1902, "The Company granted 10 acres of ground to town for burial ground per Judge Gilpin."

---

96. Ibid.

97. Holden, William Curry. *The Spur Ranch: A Study of the Inclosed Ranch Phase of the Cattle Industry in Texas* (Boston: The Christopher Publishing House, 1934), p. 180.

98. "Matador Ranch Manager's Diary, January 1-December 31-1901," The Matador Land and Cattle Company, Ltd. Collection. Southwest Collection, Texas Tech University Library, Lubbock, Texas.

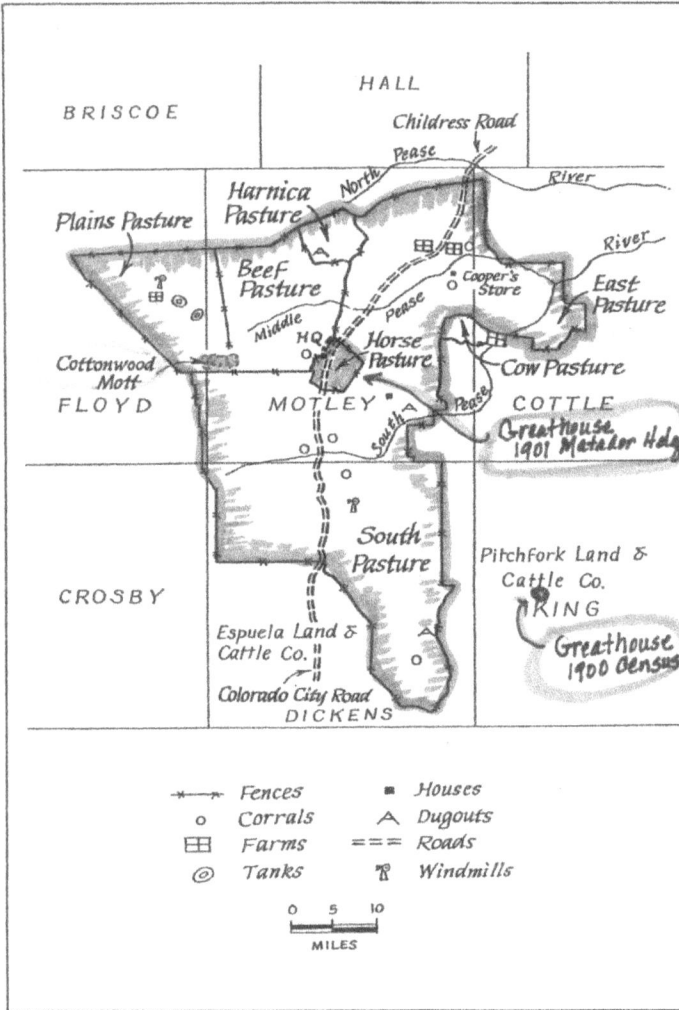

The Enclosed Range of the Matador Land and Cattle Company,
from the Survey by Sam L. Chalk in 1888

W. M. Pearce, The Matador Land and Cattle Company.
(Norman: University of Oklahoma Press, 1964.)

18. The enclosed range of the Matador Land and Cattle Company.

The managers of the Matador Land and Cattle Company were held accountable to the Scottish shareholders in Dundee, and a great deal of paperwork was accumulated, including ranch manager diaries and payroll records. In a compilation of Matador cowboy payroll records from 1883 to 1919, a "Harve" Greathouse was employed on April 19, 1888, and after he was paid $6 and $10 bounties, he was discharged.[99] No other reference to Harve has been found, but the pay was commensurate with a wolfer's pay. It is highly likely this was our subject, under an alias or registered by a faulty scribe.

Later, within a couple of years' time frame, a Matador Ranch hand, James E. Meador, told a familiar story that his son, Joe Meador, relayed to Elmer Kelton, reporter for the *Livestock Weekly* in San Angelo, Texas. The senior Meador, who hired on December 16, 1900, was healing up from a horse-related injury when he pulled cooking duty for the outfit. During his time as cook, he met a man he perceived to be a "crusty old Scot," Ridge Greathouse, who poisoned lobo wolves for the Matadors. "Every time a beef was killed at the wagon, he would pick up the offal and soak it in a tub of strychnine. Then he would drag the beef head behind his wagon to create a scent, and he would toss out poisoned baits. One day he was napping beside the chuckwagon when an irate settler came up and demanded to know his whereabouts. He shouted, 'You killed my dog. I wouldn't take $500 for that dog.' The old man gave the pilgrim one of those cotton-killing stares and said, 'You've got seven or eight hungry kids and not even a milk cow to feed them with. The last thing you needed was a $500 dog.' He (Greathouse) turned over and went back to sleep."[100]

99. Matador Ranch Cowboy List. Payroll book, 1883-1892. Southwest Collection, Texas Tech University, Lubbock, Texas. j:/public/records/mat-list.doc (printed 1994/08/01).

100. Kelton, Elmer, "James Meador," *Livestock Weekly*, San Angelo, reprinted in *the Motley County Tribune*, Matador, Texas, August 25, 1977.

If Ridge was in the vicinity during 1892-1893 when Henry H. Campbell was manager of the Matador Land and Cattle Company, the Kentuckian would have lived through a prolonged severe drought. The year before the ranch was sold to a Scottish syndicate, Campbell's son, Harry, recalled that all his school mates had moved away during that hard time, and the prairie dogs became so emaciated and docile, they became his playmates. Many years later, Harry Campbell compiled a small volume of history and added to the information about the enigmatic Ridge Greathouse with "The First Animal Trapper" of Motley County:

> Uncle Ridge Greathouse was an animal poisoner who roamed about in a little wagon following the Matador outfit. When they slaughtered a beef, they would give him the entrails and any other part they did not use. When he had put out all his poisoned baits, he would drag the entrails from one to the next, thus attracting wolves and other predatory animals for miles around. Although he was a scarecrow in appearance, those who knew him said he was a very refined man with a good education, born of a wealthy Kentucky family.
>
> He was a Forty-Niner who made a fortune, and he was a banker. Disappointed in love, he became a nomad, traveling about the world. He ran the Yankee blockade for the Confederates in his own boat and was captured, imprisoned, and escaped to wander penniless, but proud.[101]

All accounts affirm that the cowboys and settlers knew a little something of the old man's past. In that era of the frontier, few, if any, questions were asked of a man. One cowboy who worked on the Matador Ranch for years was never known by anything other than his first name; he gave no other, nor was he asked.

---

101. Campbell, Harry H. *History of Motley County* (Wichita Falls: Nortex Offset Publications, 1971), p. 41-42.

Less than a month after the Scottish-owned syndicate of the Matador Land and Cattle Company agreed to give the town of Matador 10 acres for a burying ground, Ridge passed away on April 29, 1902.[102] Although he died alone on the lone prairie, he was later joined by many of his fellow Confederates in the burying ground at East Mound. This time there would be no "miraculous escape." After 71 years, dying was the one caper from which Ridgely Greathouse could not escape.

---

102. *The Evening Bulletin*, Maysville, Kentucky. June 30, 1902.

Epilogue

A special birthday party, honoring my friend Rip Griffin of Lubbock at Hotel Matador, brought me into contact with two very special people who became champions of the subject of this biography. One guest at the party in Matador, Texas, was the lovely and gracious Wynelle Eskridge Wagnon of Lubbock.

"Do you know anything about a Ridge Greathouse?" she asked in her warm Southern drawl. The mission of my new friend was to find a Confederate grave to mark for her chapter of the United Daughters of the Confederacy (UDC). Through her friendship with the Griffins, she had heard stories about Rip's father, who had worked as a cowboy on the Matador Ranch. In addition to those stories, there was a legend about an old fellow named Ridge Greathouse, who had died on the Matador Ranch, and she thought he might qualify for the project.

Mrs. Wagnon introduced me to Danella Reno Dickson, a tireless researcher of genealogy and also a member of the Stephen W. Wilkinson Chapter of UDC. With Mrs. Dickson's help, an application was made to the UDC organization, and the chapter began to plan for a patriotic endeavor to mark the grave of Greathouse. His resting place was distinguished only by an iron Southern Cross of the Confederate States of America and a flat slab where his name had been crudely scratched in the cement.

The chapter spearheaded raising funds for a tombstone, for which Mrs. Wagnon wrote a poetic tribute denoting "The Chapman Affair of 1862." The Sons of the Confederacy provided a fitting military salute for this man with a checkered past, one who had clearly supported the Confederacy with his finances and an unfulfilled marque, but paid with his incarceration, exile, and isolation from his close-knit family.

The grave marking was just the beginning of the quest. Over the next 10 years, Mrs. Dickson embarked on an online search that she shared with the author. Utilizing newspapers, books, publications, and family histories, she followed Greathouse and his brothers through every step of their ambitious careers, finding Ridge where angels feared to tread. I consider Danella Reno Dickson's contributions absolutely essential to this history; however, any errors in the interpretation of the material belong to this author alone.

While compiling a county history, *Motley County Roundup: Over 100 Years of Gathering in Texas* (second edition, 2020), I became fascinated with the Greathouse story. I presented a research paper, "The Enigma of Ridgely Greathouse," in a conference session of the West Texas Historical Association. Newspaper articles were written, and a shortened version was published in *Stripes*, a journal of the Texas State Genealogical Society. Although this biography has been delayed in order to find as much information as possible, the story has yet to be finished.

— Marisue Burleson Potts

About the Illustrator

Kayla White is a self-taught artist who likes to experiment with different art styles. She lives in Quitaque, Texas.

Contact Kayla at kaylawhite.artist@gmail.com

Researcher's Notes

I became involved in researching Ridgely Greathouse's story by chance while volunteering in the Genealogy Department at the George and Helen Mahon Library, Lubbock, Texas. While going through a list of Confederates buried in Motley County given to me by a student researcher, I read Ridgely Greathouse's information and thought I would like to know more about him.

To avoid duplicating work done previously, I knew I needed to contact someone in the historical society in Matador, the Motley County seat. My friend, Wynelle Wagnon, advised me to contact Marisue Potts. Of course, Marisue was familiar with Mr. Greathouse's life after he arrived in the ranching area but knew little about his earlier life. I started checking census records, military records, and other common sources.

The more I learned, the more questions I had, not only about Ridgely but also his brothers, who came to California during the gold rush. I found an amazing amount of information in early newspapers. It seemed the reporters of that time found Ridgely and his brothers George and Henry fascinating, and so did I.

The early California newspapers carried extensive reports about Ridgely Greathouse's involvement with the pirate ship *Chapman*. Mr. Greathouse's arrest, imprisonment, and escape also received full coverage. Using newspaper records, I was able to follow him to Europe, to Mexico where a group of former Confederates had settled, and finally to Texas and Idaho.

This was an ongoing project for more than 10 years. Along the way, our local United Daughters of the Confederacy Chapter, with the help of the South Plains Genealogical Society and other historical groups, was able to mark the grave of Ridgely Greathouse with a proper stone. Marisue told his story to different historical groups and finally decided to preserve it by publishing a book. This gave me the opportunity to go through all the research again and try to find answers for all the questions we both still had.

We found new sources, including an interview of Mr. Greathouse in Idaho by a California newspaperman in 1868. Although it did not answer all our questions, it was reassuring to know someone tried to record his story at the time. Distant family members were contacted, and some family letters were found in publications. If anything was overlooked or missed, it was not for lack of trying.

This project has given me the opportunity to learn more about civilian life during the Civil War and how individuals could get caught up in events. I enjoyed learning more about California during the gold rush and the early days in Idaho. Genealogical research can lead a researcher down many paths and this project certainly demonstrated that.

— Danella Reno Dickson

19. Research contributor Danella Reno Dickson is surrounded by members of the South Plains Brigade of the Sons of Confederate Veterans, who dedicated a memorial to Ridgely Greathouse at East Mound Cemetery, Matador, Texas, in 2012.

20. United Sons of the Confederacy, Plemons Chapter, Amarillo, Texas, salute the memory of Ridge Greathouse.

21. Greathouse marker at East Mound Cemetery, Matador, Texas, with Dave Keith, great-grandson of P.A. Cribbs, CSA Veteran who remembered Greathouse.

Epitaph for Ridge Greathouse Marker

"The Chapman Affair of 1862"

"CAPTAIN" RIDGELY GREATHOUSE
Born: Mason Co., Kentucky 1831
Died: Matador Ranch, Texas, 1902

Here lies a once zealous,
Cultured man of Confederate Marque
Who gave his fortune and his heart
For a Southern ship that never sailed.

Dying without fanfare or honor,
He lived here in poverty and privation,
Seeking no fame or respect of person,
Capitalist to the end.

Marked at Last, 2011 A.D.

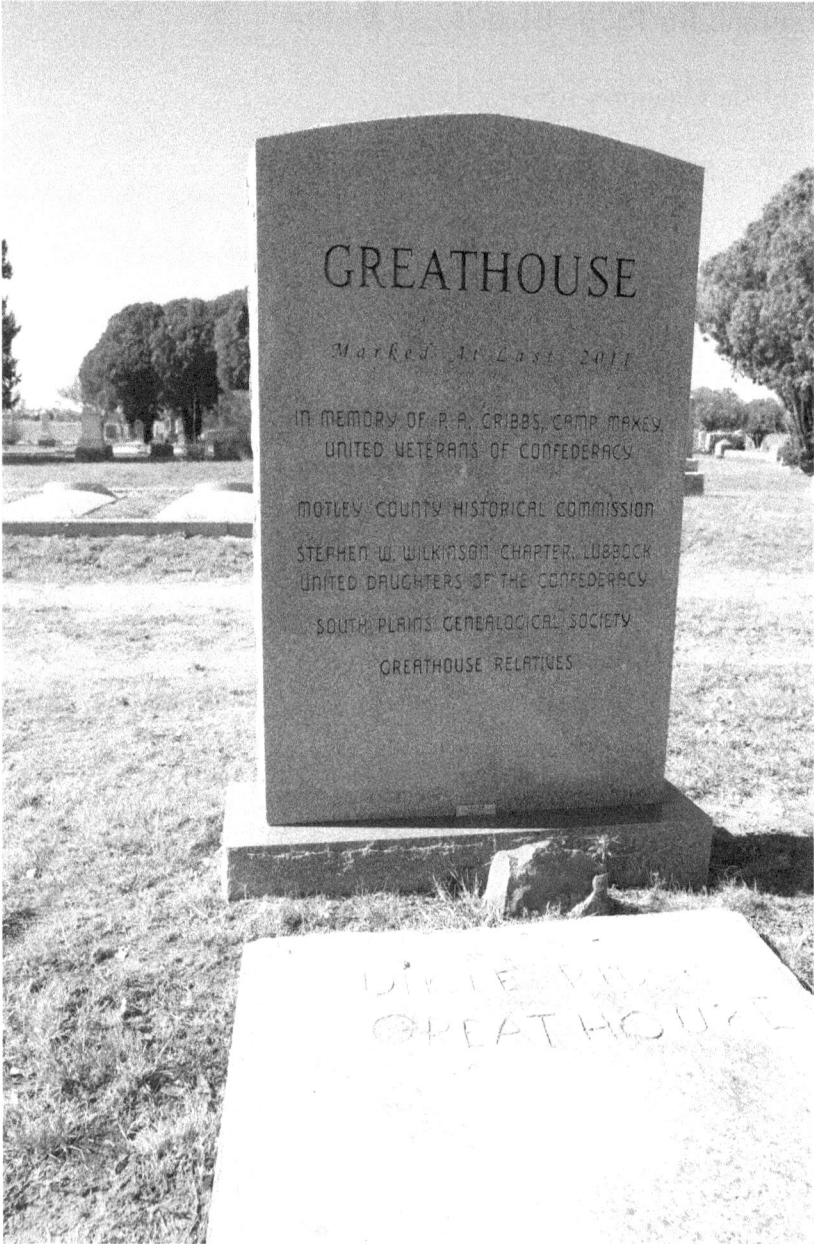

22. Greathouse marker at East Mound Cemetery showing
the hand-drawn original headstone.

Timeline for the Greathouse Brothers, 1831-2011

1831 – Ridgley Greathouse is born, the third son of Jane Lewis and William Greathouse, near Maysville, Kentucky.

1849 – Brother Henry goes to California gold fields. Their mother, Jane Lewis Greathouse, dies.

1850 – Ridgley, 19, of Mason County, Kentucky, is with brother Robert, father, William, and stepmother, Mary Forman.

1852 – George, Henry, and Ridgley, located in Yreka, Siskiyou County, California, invest in water, express, coaching, and banking.

1855 – Brothers join Hugh Slicer in daily express business from Shasta to Yreka on mountain trails.

1856 – Ridgely (name change) and servant arrive in San Francisco after the Watermelon Riot.

1861 – Kentucky trip takes Ridgely through Isthmus of Panama and meeting with Asbury Harpending.

Harpending runs through blockade to Richmond, Virginia, to seek letter of marque from Jeff Davis.

1862 – Ridgely finances and outfits a 90-ton schooner, the *J. M. Chapman,* with blank letter of marque.

1863 – Harpending, Ridgely, Alfred Rubery, and members of crew are arrested, imprisoned, and tried.

1864 – Ridgely is released under judge's ruling of President Lincoln's amnesty for British subject Rubery. He is rearrested and sent to federal prison, Fort Lafayette, New York, for swearing oaths of allegiance to the United States on 1861 Kentucky trip, which crossed Union lines twice. Ridgely escapes from prison, goes to Niagara-on-the-Lake in Canada with other Confederates in exile.

1865 – Henry and George leave California political bitterness over the Chapman Affair for Idaho mining boom and daily stage and express runs from Idaho City to Boise.

Ridgely is a guest of Rubery in England and is later seen at the Planters Hotel in Mazatlán, Mexico, where he invests in Ox Hide and Tail Hotel/Saloon with partner Dan Showalter.

1866 – Showalter argues with his former Confederate commander F.E. Kavanaugh, is wounded, and dies of lockjaw on March 4. The French Army is ordered to withdraw on May 31. Juaristas overrun the French positions and oust foreigners and Confederates.

Ridgely slips back into the United States and joins brother Robert in cattle drive to Idaho.

1867 – Maximilian is executed on June 19 in Queretaro. After cattle drive and Robert's death in Kansas, Ridgely leaves to visit Kentucky homeplace and then joins Henry and George in Idaho.

1870 – Census for Idaho City, Boise, Idaho Territory: Ridgely, 37 [39], a banker with personal property worth $17,000.

1875 – Henry and family join others in leaving Idaho for Decatur, Wise County, Texas, to buy land and settle; Henry becomes successful in banking.

1876 – Ridgely elected Door Keeper for Idaho Legislative House in Boise City.

1879 – George, with Wells Fargo once again in California, dies in Santa Rosa; Ridgely leaves Idaho.

1880 – Ridgely does not appear in records or newspapers for the next 20 years.

1900 – The census locates Ridgely in King County, Texas, 68 years old, no property, occupation: capitalist.

1901 – Ridgely is on the Matador Ranch trapping or poisoning coyotes and skinning dead cattle for pelts.

1902 – April 29, Ridgely, age 71, dies on Matador Ranch and is buried in pauper's grave.

June 20, 1902, Henry dies in Decatur, Texas, as a revered member of the community.

1925 – P.A. Cribbs petitions for a Confederate States Iron Cross marker for Ridge Greathouse.

2011 – A tombstone is placed on Ridgely Greathouse's grave and is honored with a memorial service by chapters of the United Daughters of the Confederacy and the Sons of the Confederacy.

APPENDIX B

Greathouse Genealogy

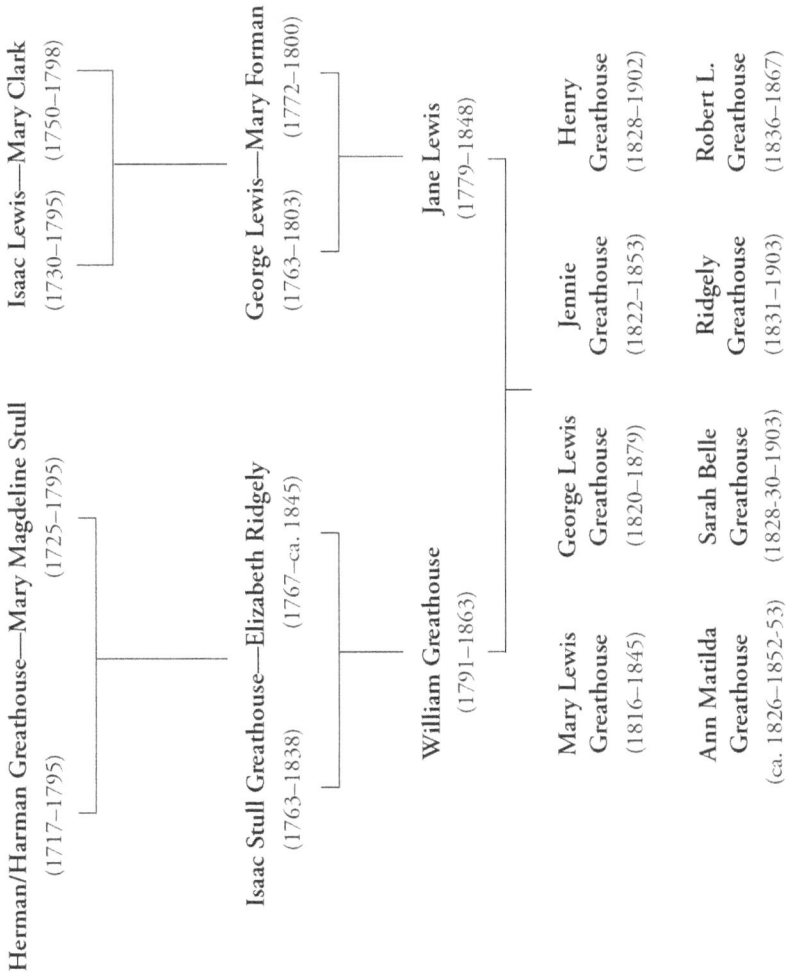

Isaac Lewis—Mary Clark
(1730–1795)   (1750–1798)

George Lewis—Mary Forman
(1763–1803)   (1772–1800)

Jane Lewis
(1779–1848)

Henry Greathouse
(1828–1902)

Robert L. Greathouse
(1836–1867)

Jennie Greathouse
(1822–1853)

Ridgely Greathouse
(1831–1903)

Herman/Harman Greathouse—Mary Magdeline Stull
(1717–1795)   (1725–1795)

Isaac Stull Greathouse—Elizabeth Ridgely
(1763–1838)   (1767–ca. 1845)

William Greathouse
(1791–1863)

George Lewis Greathouse
(1820–1879)

Sarah Belle Greathouse
(1828–30–1903)

Mary Lewis Greathouse
(1816–1845)

Ann Matilda Greathouse
(ca. 1826–1852–53)

23. Greathouse family tree. Contributed by Danella Reno Dickson.

APPENDIX C

Tradition Runs Deep

Christened with the maiden name of his grandmother, Elizabeth Ridgley Rigby, *Ridgley* Greathouse was born in 1831 in Mason County, Kentucky. His parents, William and Jane Lewis Greathouse, selected names for their sons, Ridgley and his older brother Henry, that reached back to the American Revolution. The Ridgley name first appears with Maryland colonial ancestors William Ridgley and Col. Henry Ridgley.[103] Historical identity through family names was paramount to this extended family, with the same names recurring throughout generations. Gradually, some family members, including our subject, adopted the spelling of *Ridgely*.[104]

Ridgely's eldest brother, George Lewis Greathouse, carried the name of their grandfather, Colonel George Lewis, while other members perpetuated that of their great-grandfather Isaac. A Captain Isaac Lewis, possibly related, served in Pennsylvania's Delaware

---

103. Maryland and Virginia Colonials: Genealogies of Some Colonial Families, Vol. II, Ancestry.com, Isaac Stull Greathouse Family Tree.

104. "Ridgely Greathouse" was noted in a notarized affidavit by his lawyer after the "Watermelon Riot."

County Regiment during the Revolutionary War.[105] In 1786 Colonel George Lewis, father of Jane Lewis Greathouse, settled with 50 other families on the south side of the Ohio River, where he signed a petition to form the town of Washington, Kentucky. In a few years he resettled at Clark's Station, renaming it Lewis Station, where he provided accommodations for voyagers. Lewis served as a representative to frame the Kentucky Constitution in 1792, and three years later he established Lewisburg on his 70 acres of land.[106] He also established a farm in distant Christian County, located in the northwestern corner of Kentucky.

The Greathouse family had its own history to recount through names. The original spelling of Groethausen came to America from Germany with Harmon (1670–1743), who died in Pennsylvania. As the growing family branched out to Maryland, Georgia, and Kentucky in the Northwest Territory, the Groethausens became Americanized and adopted the name of "Greathouse."

With the third generation in America, blacksmith Harmon Groethausen married Mary Magdalena Stull. Their male children included Daniel, Jacob, John, William, Gabriel, Harmon, Jr., Isaac Stull (our subject's line), and Jonathan. Recruited during the War of the Revolution from Washington County, Pennsylvania, were the American-born sons of Harmon and Mary Stull. William served in the Washington County militia while Colonel Harmon Groethausen, Jr., served in the Rangers with the Frontier Regiment,

---

105. Pennsylvania, Delaware County, Regiment, Revolutionary War 1777-1780. Isaac Lewis recruited by Capt. Enoch Anderson (p. 26), Dead or Deserted list, January 23, 1777. https://www.fold3.com/

106. Clift, G. Glenn. *History of Maysville and Mason County, Kentucky* (Lexington: Transylvania Printing, 1936), pp. 56, 78, 110, 122.

repelling Indian attacks and later defending the Continental Line[107] for the Continental Army rebels.

A Jacob Groethausen (possibly from this family, but unproven to date) served in the Continental Army in 1776. Its newly formed German Regiment was comprised of 450 men who distinguished themselves by crossing the Delaware with George Washington on Christmas Eve, 1776, under dire circumstances. Recruited in Pennsylvania but short on supplies and equipment, the German-American unit marched to the Battle of Trenton through freezing hail, rain, and sleet to surprise the British and their auxiliary Hessian troops. Cutting off the possibility of retreat, the second- or third-generation Americans cried out in their native language to the German mercenaries, thereby enticing three Hessian regiments to surrender. After facing several defeats, illnesses, lack of pay, scanty rations, and the defection or capture of their regiment commander, the men suffered frustration and low morale. The shorter enlistment period changed from several months to three years, or the duration of the war. In 1777, Jacob was listed as "deserted," however, family accounts record the death of Jacob that year. Likewise, some 53 sick and 17 furloughed men also did not return to serve out the long term that earned them only a bounty of $10.[108]

Another son of Harmon, Sr., John served with the 8th Pennsylvania Regiment, assigned to the Northern Department of the Continental Army, which saw action in New York, New Jersey,

107. Greathouse, Jack Murray, "A Partial History of The Greathouse Family in America," No. 7 in the Bulletin Series. (Fayetteville, Arkansas: Washington County Historical Society, 1954), p. 43.

108. Weaver, John B., "A Corps of Much Service, The German Regiment of the Continental Army." (Undergraduate Honors Theses, William & Mary, 2017), https://scholarworks.wm.edu/honorstheses/1050.

and Philadelphia. For serving throughout the war, John was awarded a federal pension.[109]

The draw for the youngest Groethausen brother, Jonathan, was the Ohio River Frontier. He was only 11 years old during the Revolutionary War, when his older brothers were fighting the British. The Americanized Captain Jonathan Greathouse[110] was on his way to the village of Limestone in Mason County on March 24, 1791, with a festive party of settlers. While traveling down the major transportation corridor of the Ohio River, their slow-moving flatboats, powered only by oars, were attacked by Indians. A defense formed and a fight ensued. The attack was apparently in retaliation for the participation of Jonathan's older brother, Daniel Greathouse, in the Yellow Creek Massacre during Lord Dunmore's War of 1774.[111] That battle resulted in the killing of the family of James Logan, war leader of the Iroquois-allied Mingo tribe. Ten days after the assault, Greathouse and his intended bride, Henrietta Rigby, were found on the riverbank, naked, with his entrails strung out on saplings and her body ravaged by hogs. With General Anthony Wayne subduing the Iroquois by 1794, this was the last recorded attack staged on flatboats on the Ohio.[112]

---

109. Greathouse, Jack Murray, "A Partial History of The Greathouse Family in America," No. 7 in the Bulletin Series. (Fayetteville, Arkansas: Washington County Historical Society, 1954), p. 43.

110. "Jonathan Greathouse (1766-1791)," "Gabriel Greathouse (1761-1829)," Ancestry Family Trees, Provo, Utah, ancestry.com.

111. "Lord Dunmore's War—1774" and "James Logan, American Indian Leader," *Encyclopaedia Britannica*, accessed on April 18, 2020: https://www.britannica.com/event/Lord-Dunmores-War; https://www.britannica.com/biography/James-Logan-American-Indian-leader

112. Clift, G. Glenn. *History of Maysville and Mason County, Kentucky*, Vol. 1 (Lexington: Transylvania Printing Co., 1936), pp. 103-106.

APPENDIX D

Crew for the *J.M. Chapman* Pirate Ship

Stockton Daily Independent, March 16-21, 1863

1. Ridgely Greathouse, ostensible owner
2. Asbury Harpending, native of Kentucky
3. Alfred Rubery, an Englishman, passenger
4. W.W. Mason, Alabama
5. Albion T. Crow, Confederacy
6. John E. Kent, Illinois
7. Wm. C. Law, New York, Commander
8. Lorenzo L. Libby (Libbie), First Officer
9. Thomas Reole, Kentucky
10. Joseph W. Smith, aka Snyder, Kentucky
11. Alfred Armond, Ottawa, Canada West
12. Henry C. Boyd, Delaware
13. R.H. Duval, Florida
14. Wm. D. Moore
15. J.W. McFadden
16. Wm. W. Maron (Mason)

17. D.W. Brown
18. John Fletcher
19. James Smith
20. George W. Davis
21. M.H. Marshall
22. Personnel, including five sailors, cook, steward, and etc.

Bibliography

Bailey, Christopher H. *The Stulls of "Millsborough," A Genealogical History of John Stull "The Miller," Pioneer of Western Maryland*, Vol. 1 (C.H. Bailey; limited first edition, January 2000), Descendants of (Col.) John Stull of Hagerstown, Mary (Stull) Greathouse and Margaret (Stull) White. Also can be viewed online at https://www.familysearch.org/library/books/records/item/420731-redirection

Burlingame, Michael, ed. *Lincoln Observed, Civil War Dispatches of Noah Brooks* (Baltimore and London: The Johns Hopkins University Press, 1998).

Campbell, Harry H. *The Early History of Motley County* (Wichita Falls: Nortex Offset Publications, 1971).

Clift, G. Glenn. *History of Maysville and Mason County, Kentucky*, Vol. 1 (Lexington: Transylvania Printing Co., 1936).

Collinson, Frank. *Life in the Saddle* (Norman: University of Oklahoma Press, 1963).

Daniel, Clinton, Editor. *Chronicle of America* (Mount Kisco, NY: Chronicle Publications, 1989).

Davis, Edwin Adams. *Fallen Guidon, The Saga of Confederate General Jo Shelby's March to Mexico* (College Station: Texas A&M University Press, 1995).

Fulton, Arabella Clemens. *Tales of the Trail* (Caldwell: B. C. Payette, 1965; Decatur, Texas: Wise County Heritage Museum).

Gilbert, Benjamin Franklin, "Kentucky Privateers in California." *Kentucky State Historical Society*, Vol. 38. No. 124.

Green, John Duff. *Recollections* (Roaring Springs, Texas: Joan Green Lawrence, editor, 1988).

Harpending, Asbury. *The Great Diamond Hoax and Other Stirring Incidents in the Life of Asbury Harpending* (San Francisco: The James H. Barry Co., 1913). Online reproduction can be found at http://www.books-about-california.com/Pages/The_Great_Diamond_Hoax/

Holden, William Curry. *The Spur Ranch: A Study of the Inclosed Ranch Phase of the Cattle Industry in Texas* (Boston: The Christopher Publishing House, 1934).

Hunter, J. Marvin. *The Trail Drivers of Texas* (Austin: University of Texas Press, 1985).

King County Historical Commission. *King County Windmills & Barbed Wire* (Quanah: Nortex Press, 1976).

Lowe, Richard, and Ronald Marcello, co-editors. *Military History of the Southwest*, Vol. 19, spring 1989, No. 1 (Denton: University of North Texas, 1989).

O'Meara, James O., "A Notable Escape," *The Californian,* San Francisco, Vol. 28, April 1882. [Note this includes information from an 1868 interview of Ridgely Greathouse.]

Rescher, Nicholas. *The Niagara [Ontario] Historical Society* (Fox Chapel, Pennsylvania: NAP Publications, 2003).

Robinson, William Morrison, Jr. *The Confederate Privateers* (Columbia, South Carolina: University of South Carolina Press, 1990).

Rolle, Andrew. *The Lost Cause, The Confederate Exodus to Mexico* (Norman and London: University of Oklahoma, 1965).

Traweek, Eleanor Mitchell. *Of Such as These, a History of Motley County, Texas* (Quanah, Wichita Falls: Nortex Publications, 1973).

Online Articles

Chandler, Robert J., "The Greathouse Brothers & Slicer's Express," *Western Express, Research Journal of Early Western Mails*, Vol. 46, No. 1, March 1996. Western Cover Society, 1996. https://www.westerncoversociety.org/wp-content/uploads/2017/05/Western_Cover_Society__Western_Express__1996-03.pdf

Early Settlement of Idaho, Access Genealogy. 1999-2011. http://accessgenealogy.com/idaho/early_settlement_of_idaho.htm

Robinson, W.W., editor. *The Westerners Brand Book #7* (Los Angeles: Corral of Westerners, 1957), article by George E. Fullerton: "The Fabulous Greathouse Brothers." http://www.lawesterners.org/2013/08/09/the-westerners-brand-book-7-1957/

Howe, Edward H. and Benjamin F. Gilbert. "Land and Labor in Kentucky," 1865; Letters to George Lewis Greathouse. *The Register of the Kentucky Historical Society*, Vol. 48, No. 162 (January 1950), pp. 25-31. Kentucky Historical Society, 1950. https://www.jstor.org/stable/i23372608

K.G.C. An authentic exposition of the origin, objects, and secret work of the organization known as the Knights of the Golden Circle. http://quod.lib.umich.edu/cgi/t/text/text-idx?c=moa;cc=moa;rgn=main;view

Knights of the Golden Circle. http://knightsofthegoldencircle.webs.com

About the Author

Born in Matador, Texas, Marisue Burleson Potts grew up on a ranch where her father and grandfather ran herds of Hereford cattle. A 1960 graduate of Floydada High School, Floydada, Texas, she graduated from Texas Tech University in 1998 after the last of her five children had graduated from the Lubbock institution. She has served as Motley County Historical Commission chairman and a founding board member of the Motley County Historical Museum, Matador; the Comanchero Canyons Museum, Quitaque, Texas; and the Canyonlands Archeological Society of Matador and Quitaque. During 2012-2013, she served as president of the West Texas Historical Association of Lubbock, Texas, and has made presentations of a historical nature at their annual conferences, as well as other heritage organizations. Her articles have been published in the *Motley County Tribune,* the *Valley Tribune,* the *Caprock Courier,* the *Texas Techsan Ex-Students Magazine,* the *Lubbock Avalanche Journal,* and the National Cowboy Symposium's *Catch Pen.* She is the author of *Motley County Roundup: Over 100 Years of Gathering in Texas* (Mollie Burleson Ranch Ltd., 2020).

Deserted to the Wind

The sun, obscured by boiling clouds of red dust, casts an eerie, unnatural light on the deserted farmstead. Swirls of sand whip around the empty buildings.

The wind sweeps the hard crust of the lot, whisking away any sign of the manure that once blanketed the ground. The shy loft door is coaxed open, then when rejected, protests with an incessant bang, bang, bang.

Wind-hurled pebbles ping against the rusty tin roof of the saddle shed where pack rats hoard their treasures of cow chips, shiny wrappers, and tin lids. Horseshoes huddle beneath the floor where they leaped to freedom through a crack.

Gawking like a toothless old hag, the outhouse immodestly reveals her musty secrets. Within, the water-stained roll of paper twists and turns on its way to the dusty floor, unfurled by the same prying, poking wind.

In the overgrown yard, a weathered gate swings to and fro, keeping time to an unheard melody. Bare tree roots claw at the parched earth, desperately seeking something, anything. Challenging the wind's demanding caresses, the dry, brittle weeds rattle and shake like an angry rattlesnake.

The house door stands ajar as if someone stepped out to gather the eggs but forgot to return. Only silence and a billowy curtain greet me.

Melancholy sweeps over me like the wind. What stories has this house witnessed, never to be told? I weep for the things that were and are no more.

— Marisue Burleson Potts, 1971

Index

www.ingramcontent.com/pod-product-compliance
Lightning Source LLC
Chambersburg PA
CBHW022011090426

42741CB00007B/978